"MINNESOTA FATS"
on POOL

The complete guide for the Pool Enthusiast

Rules, Illustrations, Complete and Easy to Understand Directions

First Printing Feb. 1965
Second Printing April 1968

Printed in the U.S.A.

TABLE OF CONTENTS

To my wife Evelyn

HE SHOT OUT THE LIGHTS . . . .

In the chancy realm of cue and ivory,
    There reigns a king, rotund and lively,
His fame and frame spread far and wide,
    For quick is his stick and fierce his pride,
He sets 'em up and he cracks 'em out
    And wins the cash in bout after bout.

Now New York Fats was his poolroom name,
    'Til Hollywood gave him lasting fame,
His stroke is feared both near and far
    In Hong Kong, Rio and Zanzibar
And the warning's out in North Dakota,
    Beware, beware of Old Minnesota.

The Flick was swell, a fabulous story,
    Exposing Old Fats in all his glory,
The eighth great wonder he has been called,
    When he's off on a run of nine jillion balls,
For on the table he has no peer,
    He whacks 'em out and they run like deer.

Every last hustler he's seen come and go,
    Vanquished by cue or braggadocio,
He beats 'em all like an old bass drum,
    And always for cash, not ever for fun,
Immodest he is, shy he is not,
    But there isn't a shot Fats hasn't shot.

In any session that you can name,
    Fatty will boast he won every game,
Nine ball, black ball or pocket apiece,
    Fats and the cash go east with the geese,
I've seen him play and this much I know
    There was never a shot that Fatty did blow.

When the game's over and Fatty's gone home,
    To settle the tab at the golden throne,
Before he clears the gates of admission,
    He'll pitch St. Pete a quick proposition,
Let's have no more jolts and let's have no fights,
    Just write in your book—Fats shot out the lights.

A VICTIM—1963

A Personal Note from
"Minnesota Fats"

Welcome to the fascinating world of pool. I have spent all of my life playing the various games that are possible on a pool table and I'm never over the spectacular interest there is in the game.

Any game played on a pool table requires skill. The luckiest person in the world can lose at a pool table if they don't have the necessary skill to play the game.

This book, in which I explain the various fundamentals and rules of the many games, should be helpful to both the beginner and the oldtime pool player. I have tried my best to make the instructions so that you may grasp the fundamentals of each game. Of course, playing the game will give the best application of the rules.

Sometimes the rules for a game are easy to put on paper, but difficult to interpret when a game is in progress. This may be the case with some of the rules included in this book. It is also possible that a dispute may arise over an unusual situation or game not covered in these pages.

Should you ever have any questions about games, rules, cue sticks or table equipment, I sincerely invite you to write me for the answer.

My address is:
Minnesota Fats Enterprises
6501 North Lincoln Avenue
Lincolnwood, Illinois 60645
Cordially,
Minnesota Fats

Minnesota Fats

The Fundamentals of Pool

"Practice makes perfect" is as true in pool as in anything else. In order to make your practice time worth while I'm going to try and pass on to you some of the fundamentals that all top players have mastered. Everyone, of course, is a different individual and may, in time, develop slightly different ways of doing things but as a rule most new players start with and develop bad habits in form. To these players I say, practice perfect execution of the tips that follow and see what happens. It's truly amazing how much your game will improve by learning to make a proper bridge or developing a smooth natural stroke and follow through or correcting any mistake in technique.

To sum things up . . . . examine your own habits, compare them with my recommendations and finally practice, practice, practice.

Sincerely,
Minnesota Fats

Minnesota Fats

Cue Selection and Grip

Regulation length cues are 57″ long. There are also 52″ and 48″ cues for bumper pool tables, children or tight spots in the home. Cues used on the larger snooker tables are 60″ long.

Almost all of the cues used by adults today are 57″ long and weigh between 15 and 22 oz. The diameter of the shaft at the tip runs from 11 to 14 millimeters. The great majority of 57″ cues fall

Figure 1

Figure 2

between 18 and 20 oz. with 12 or 13 millimeter tips. I, myself use a 20 oz. cue with 13 millimeter shaft but have seen players ⅓ my size shoot a great game with a 22 oz. "club". It all goes to show that personal taste and "feel" are all important in choosing a cue.

Be sure that you have straight cues. Determine this by sighting down the cue like a rifle. Rolling the cue on the table is really unfair to the cue as most popular priced cues are not "turned" with great precision. Upon rolling, it may appear warped because of the high spots but in reality the cue may be straight as an arrow.

A cue should be gripped about a "hand" (approximately 4 inches inches) behind the balance point. Locate the balance point by laying the cue across the fingers as in figure 1. Slide the cue along your fingers until the cue balances. This is the balance point. It is not wise to hold the cue much farther back unless you have to reach a moderately long shot.

Last but not least—hold the cue lightly . . . don't strangle it. Hold the cue with your thumb and 3 fingers only while not letting the butt of the cue contact the palm of your hand. With this type of grip you will have much more control over your game.

Proper Stance:

As in any sport, players develop different basic positions but most top players stick closely to the following pattern: (Figure 2) Stand about 1 foot from the table with your right foot in line with the cue ball.

4

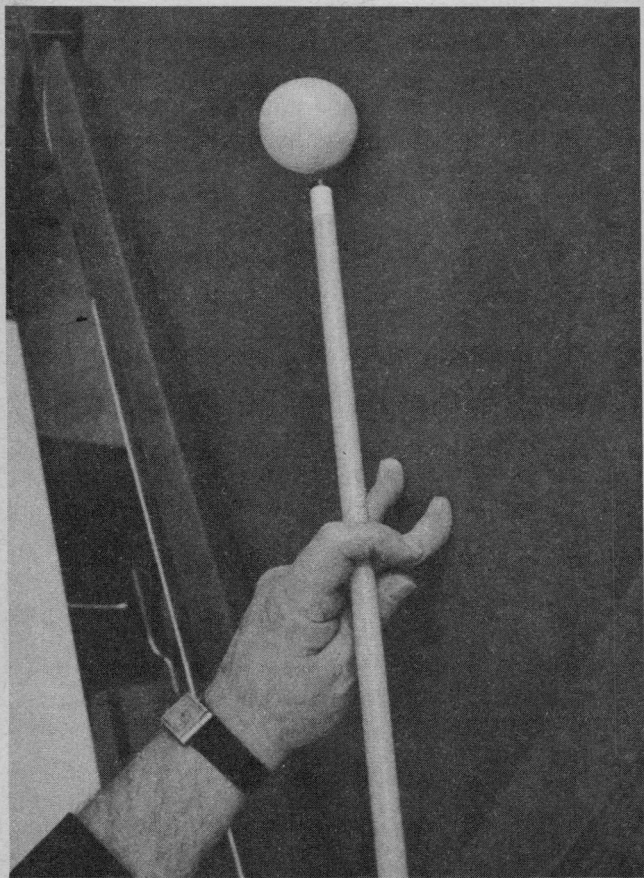

Figure 3

Face the direction of your shot with your head over the cue in the line of aim.

Turn your left foot slightly to the right. Move your right foot back until the toe of your right foot is opposite the middle of your life foot. Be sure to distribute your weight evenly on both feet. Your left arm should be extended, with the slightest bend at the elbow, straight to the bridge position. The proper stance can make the difference between a good player and a terrific one. Be sure to practice your stance, as outlined above, until it becomes second nature to you.

Making A Bridge:

Here is the downfall of many new players. An improper bridge that doesn't firmly control the shaft of the cue can ruin everything.

Almost every top player uses the "tripod" bridge (Figure 3). Notice that the first finger is looped around the shaft forming a cylinder for the cue between the thumb and side of the hand. Some players prefer to keep the base of their hand on the table for support and some are more comfortable doing it the way I've shown in the illustration.

The bridge should be made firmly yet allow the cue to slide smoothly. Here is where a good grade of billiard talc is indispensable. A light dusting of talc on the fingers of the bridge hand will absorb moisture and allow the shaft to glide more smoothly. It is also helpful to keep your cue clean and free from grime by occasionally wiping the shaft down with extra fine steel wool.

In all cases the distance between the tip of the cue shouldn't exceed 8 inches unless an unusual

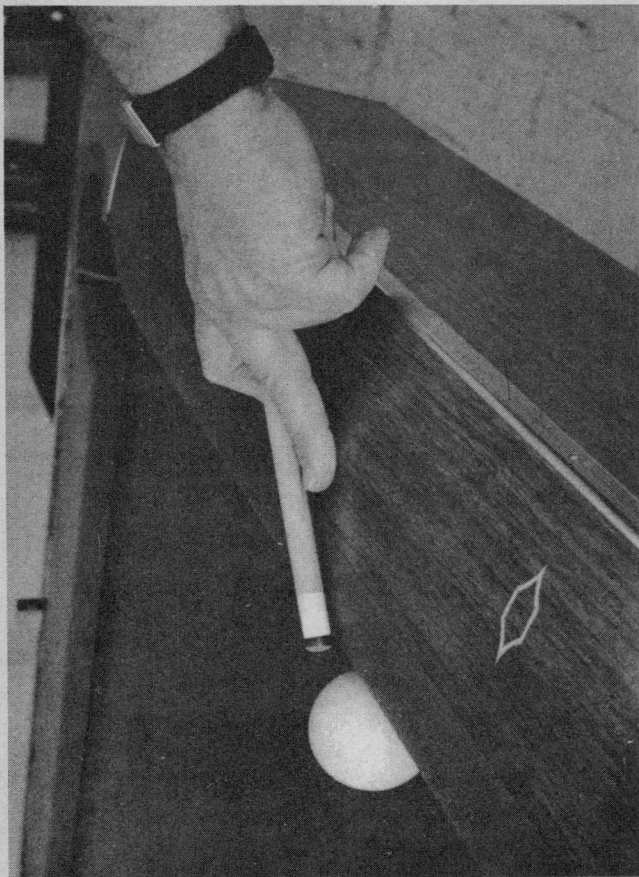

Figure 4

Figure 5

shot is necessary. When cue ball is near or frozen to the cushion, form a bridge or guide for the cue with the first two fingers (Figure 4). In this bridge the cue rests and slides on the top surface of the cushion with the 2 fingers directing the path to the cue ball.

In some types of shots where the cue ball is near or frozen to the cushion it is more comfortable to use a "tripod" bridge on the rail.

Experience will tell you which is best.

The Bridge "Stick"

The mechanical bridge commonly known as the "bridge stick" is absolutely necessary for those long shots where one foot cannot be kept on the floor.

When placing the bridge on the table, be careful not to foul by disturbing a ball. Place the bridge firmly on the table at an angle to the line of shooting (Figure 5). Grip the butt of the cue as shown.

It is important in these shots to keep your eye on the ball, mind on what you are doing, and not take anything for granted. Shots with a bridge stick should be easy most of the time but I've seen many good players miss these shots because they were cocky.

Stroke and Follow Through

A good stroke and follow through seem to be a natural asset of some players while some have to practice it dilligently. It is worth long, hard practice because you cannot shoot accurately with a tense, short, choppy stroke.

A good stroke requires the proper firm yet relaxed grip on the cue (Figure 6), and proper stance

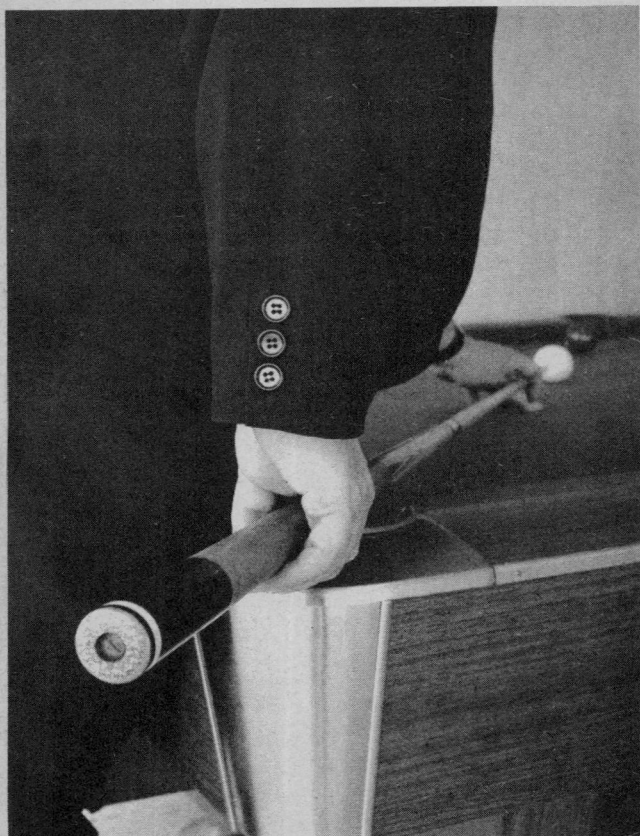

Figure 6

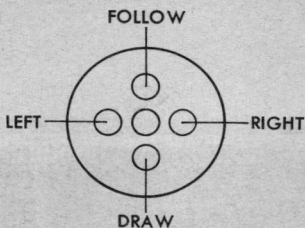

Figure 7

Figure A—Proper approach for follow shot.

Figure B—Proper approach for draw shot.

Figure C—Proper approach for center ball.

at the table. Allow your arm to swing easily and freely from the elbow—somewhat like the pendulum on a clock. Now, most important, control the cue and continue the stroke after hitting the cue ball. This is the follow through. Make your follow through smooth, sure and rhythmic. Never forget that a good follow through is as important in pool as it is in golf or baseball.

Hitting the Cue Ball

Now you're ready for the most important fundamental of all . . . learning to make the cue ball work *for* you.

Most shots, perhaps 80%, can be made using a center ball hit; that is, contacting the cue ball directly in the center (Figure 7). On a center ball hit, the cue ball will act and rebound "true." The term "English" refers to a spinning motion imparted to the cue ball by hitting the cue ball off center. This "English" causes the cue ball to rebound from its object into the direction of its spin.

For example, if you want the cue ball to move to the left after contact with the object, hit the ball to the left of center. "Draw" or "follow" is accomplished by striking the cue ball low or high respectively. Proper approaches are illustrated in figures A, B, and C.

English is necessary when playing position or making certain shots. The degree of English can be varied according to where you hit the cue ball. The general rule though is to not hit the cue ball more than a cue tip's diameter away from center.

The condition of your cue tip is of extreme importance when using English. The tip must be crowned properly, "loose" (roughed slightly with sand paper) and well chalked. Keeping your tip in this condition will help you control the cue ball and cut down on miscues. Much practice should go into hitting the ball properly. Methods of practice are described below.

Center Ball Practice:
Place cue ball on head spot. Try to hit ball so that it goes over the foot spot and hits the center diamond on the foot rail. Ball should rebound back over the foot spot and head spot.

Right and Left English:
Place cue ball on head spot. Shoot at center diamond on foot rail using right or left hand English. Note the balls action off the cushion as you vary the amount of English applied. Practice this from varying distances and with different "speeds."

Draw and Follow:
Place cue ball on head spot. Place object ball approximately 12 to 18″ away on angle towards far corner pocket. Practice pocketing object ball while hitting cue ball high or low and note results. Also practice hitting the cue ball high or low with English to the left or right while mixing speeds.

Be sure at all times to keep the cue as level as possible. Alter the height of your bridge for a low or high ball hit but always try to keep the cue on a level plane.

PART TWO

Shotmaking

Taking Aim:

The rule in pool, just as in other sports, is keep your eye on the ball. As you approach a shot you must mentally "set up" the shot deciding where you want to hit the object ball and where you want to hit the cue ball. As you approach the cue ball and make your bridge you are actually aiming at 2 balls.

As you take your warm-up strokes, take careful aim first at the object then at the cue ball. Warm up until you feel "in the grove." Your attention should switch to the point of aim on the object ball as you stroke.

It is sometimes difficult for beginners to concentrate on the two balls properly but it must be mastered if you wish to be a top player. Take as many warm-up strokes as you like. Some top players will take up to 10 or more. I, myself, usually take 3 or 4.

Basic Shots: Straight Ins and Angles

The most basic shot in pool is, of course, the "straight-in" shot where the cue ball and object ball are in a direct line to the pocket. There is not

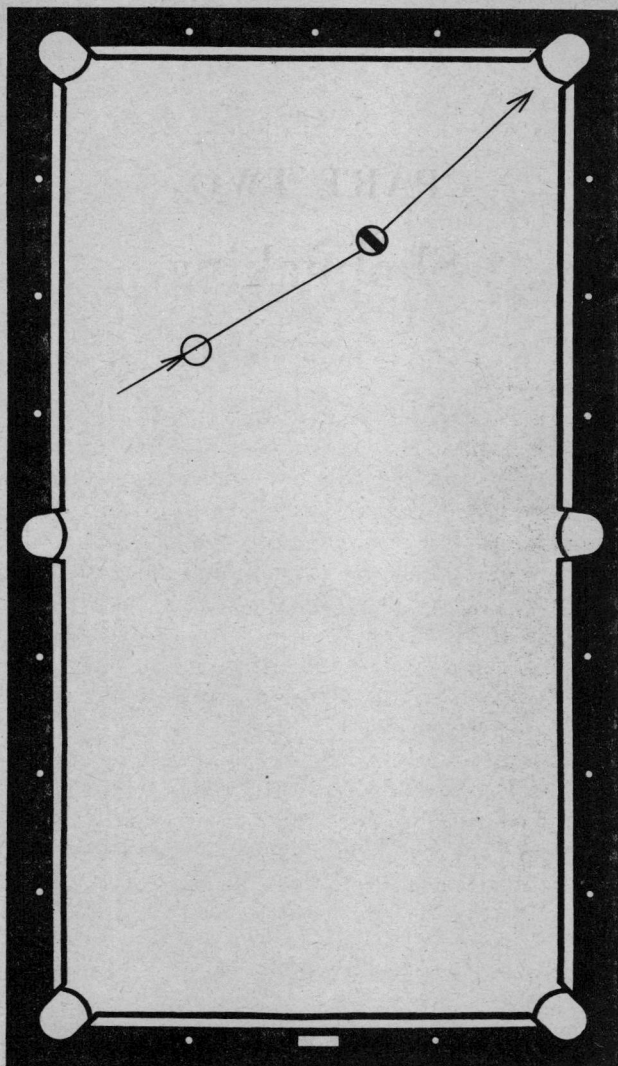

Figure 8

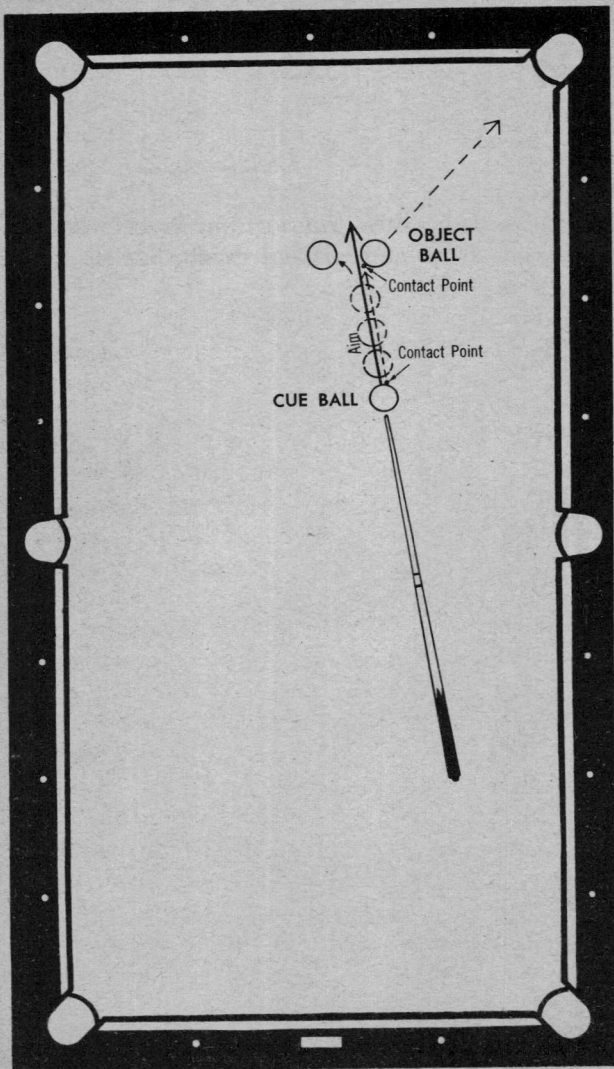

OBJECT BALL

Contact Point

Aim

Contact Point

CUE BALL

Figure 9

much to say about simple straight-ins except that you must compensate if English is to be applied to the cue ball. A cue ball, say with right hand English on it, will cause the object ball to drift slightly to the left. A good player must always keep this in mind and practice his straight-ins. They are as basic yet crucial to a winning game as free throws are in basketball or field goals in football.

The great majority of shots in pool will be "angle shots." That is the shot where the cue ball must strike the object ball a certain amount off center to drive it at an angle straight into the pocket. (Figure 8.)

In sizing up an angle shot you must decide the angle and path of the ball. To do this first draw an imaginary line from the center of the pocket through the center of the object ball. Draw another imaginary line from the cue ball to the object ball at the point where the imaginary line would exit the object ball (on the side away from the pocket), this is your point of aim. Now, most important, you must allow for the curvature of the ball. This means that you must aim so that the cue ball actually *meets* the object ball at the point of aim. (As in Figure 9.) You can see that if the cue and cue ball were aimed directly at the contact point the balls would meet before the desired spot and direct the object ball away from the pocket.

Here again I remind you to practice, practice, practice until all is second nature to you.

Ball Frozen On Rail:

This is a situation that arises in a game and bears

17

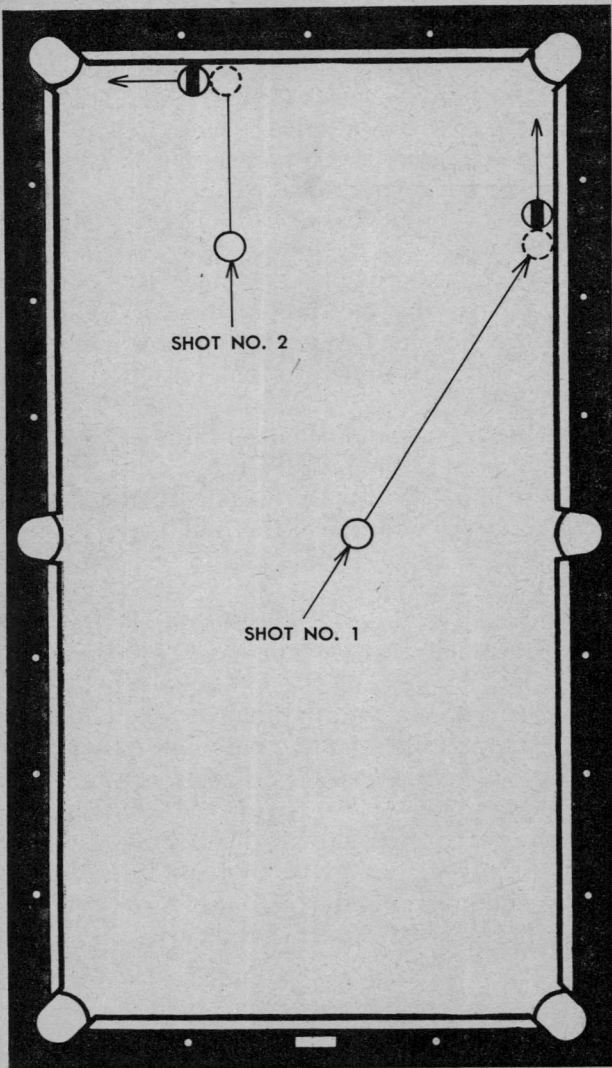

SHOT NO. 2

SHOT NO. 1

Figure 10

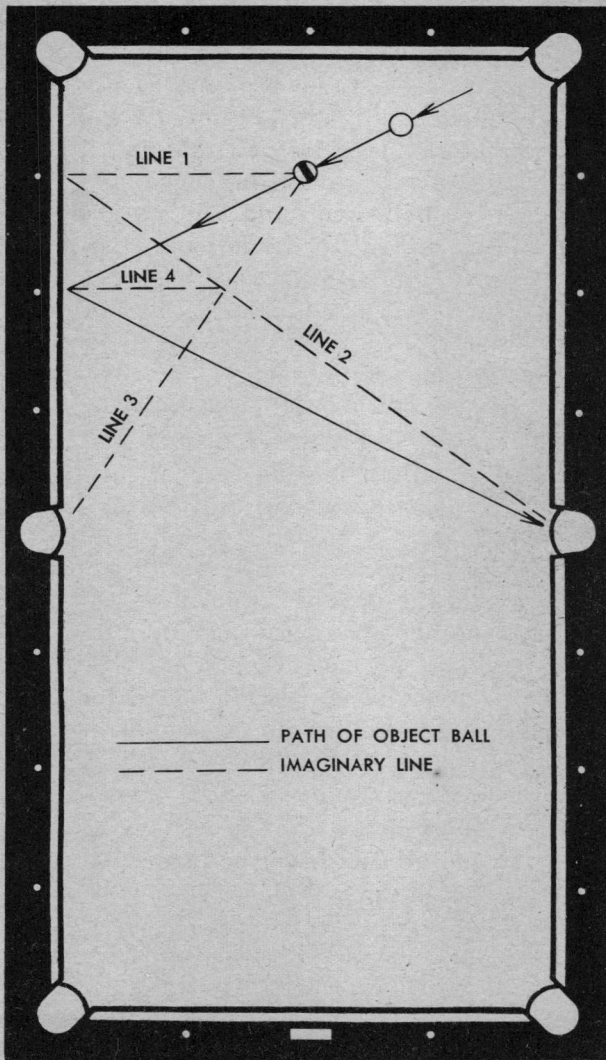

LINE 1

LINE 4

LINE 2

LINE 3

PATH OF OBJECT BALL

IMAGINARY LINE

Figure 11

discussing. This shot seems to mystify many new players but is really easy once you know what to do.

The secret here is to hit the object ball and the cushion at the same time. (Figure 10, shot #1.) When in position as shot #2 (Figure 10), you must aim to barely graze the object ball while giving the cue ball right hand English so that the object ball is thrown to the left into the pocket.

Bank Shots:

A player without a thorough knowledge of the bank shot will always be in trouble when he doesn't have to be. Figure 11 illustrates a typical bank shot situation. In this case or any similar situation you should line up the shot as follows:

a. Draw an imaginary line from the object ball directly to the far rail. (Line 1.)
b. Draw another imaginary line from that point to the object pocket. (Line 2.)
c. Now draw an imaginary line from the object ball to the pocket on the far side of the table. (Line 3.)
d. At the point where lines 2 and 3 intersect, draw an imaginary line to the far cushion. (Line 4.) You should aim to drive the object ball to the cushion at the point where line 4 terminates.

Use a crisp, medium hard stroke and a center cue ball hit on most bank shots. After a good deal of bank shot practice the above will all become second nature.

The "Pool" Table

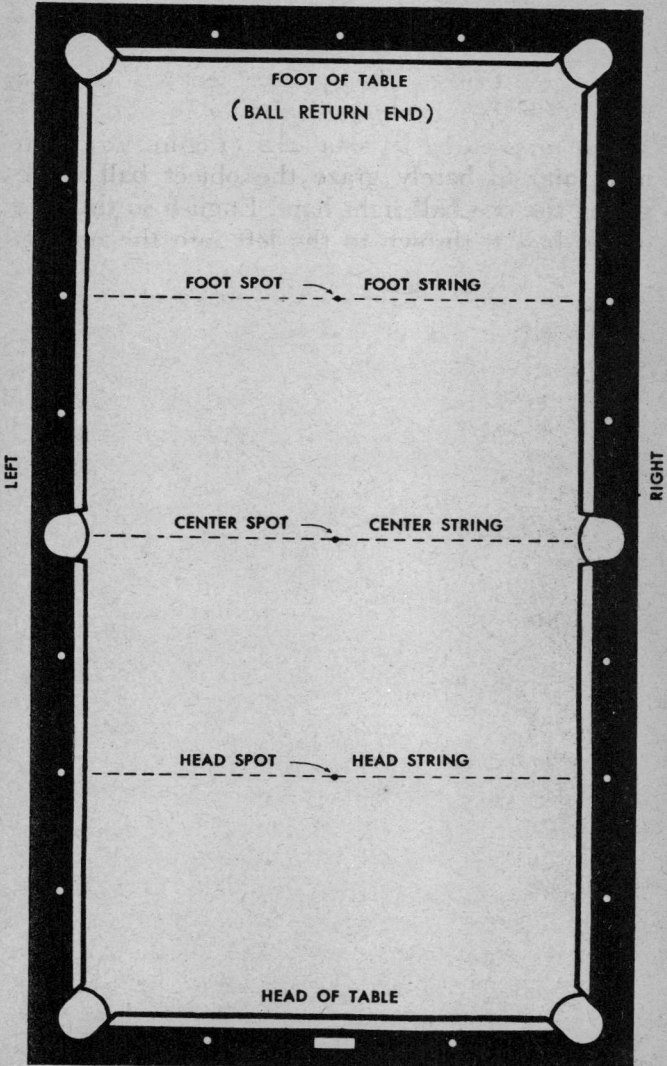

Figure 12

Game Rules for Pool

The worst crime today is calling "pool" pocket billiards. The term "pocket billiards" was coined in an attempt to improve the image of pool but there's no getting around the facts, pool is pool and billiards is billiards.

Basic "pool"

This game requires the fifteen object balls racked on the foot spot in the standard fashion. (Figure 12.) This is a good game for individuals or teams of two. The primary object of this game is for one team to pocket eight of the fifteen balls before his opponents.

Beginning player is determined by lagging or the flip of a coin. The individual starting play has cue ball in hand and may break from any point behind the head string. His first stroke must pocket a ball or drive two object balls to a cushion. In tournament play when this is not accomplished the opponent has a choice of accepting the balls in position or insisting that the balls be reracked and that the opening player repeat his break shot until this rule is fulfilled. "Call" of the opening shot is not necessary and player is credited with all balls legally pocketed.

On all succeeding plays following the opening

stroke the player must call the ball he intends to pocket, however he is not compelled to call the pocket. If a called ball is not pocketed other balls which have accidentally been pocketed on that stroke do not count. These balls must be spotted and the player loses his turn but with no penalty.

When a player calls more than one ball, all must be pocketed. If all called balls are not pocketed no ball pocketed is counted. These balls must be spotted up with player losing turn and no penalty. When a player pockets the ball he has called he is entitled to all other balls pocketed on the same stroke.

On each stroke succeeding the opening stroke the player must either pocket his called ball, drive an object ball to a cushion or drive the cue ball to a cushion after hitting an object ball.

Fouls:
1. Not complying with break shot requirements. One point is lost for each failure.
2. Scratching a cue ball in a pocket.
3. Shooting the cue ball off the table.
4. Shooting when balls are in motion.
5. Failure during play to pocket a ball, drive an object ball to a cushion or cause cue ball to contact cushion after hitting object ball.
6. For hitting cue ball twice on same stroke.
7. Touching object or cue ball with hands, cue stick, clothing or other object except on a legal stroke with the cue.

Penalties for the above fouls are imposed by the offending player forfeiting a ball for each foul in addition to those pocketed on the foul stroke. If the offending player has no balls to his credit when committing a foul he then owes the ball to the table which must be spotted when he scores. When scoring two fouls on one stroke only one penalty is imposed.

If balls are illegally interfered with by the player at the table the incoming player may elect to accept them in position or demand that the original position of balls be restored. If a player scores interference while his opponent is in the process of shooting the offending player loses the game.

If balls are disturbed by any person or factor other than the players, conditions are restored to those before the disturbance with player continuing his inning.

"One Pocket" or "Pocket Apiece"

This is the game for top players, combining the toughest aspects of billiards and pool into the most difficult of games played on a pocket table. "One pocket" requires proficiency in bank shots, English and position play.

The primary object of this game is to put eight balls into the one pocket at the foot of the table designated as the players pocket. The choice of pockets is left to the winner of the break. Conventional methods are used to choose the player who breaks. Balls are racked at the foot spot in no particular order.

On the "break" the object or cue ball must touch a rail for safety.

A ball which falls into the players pocket or his opponents pocket is a score. A score is made no matter which player was responsible for putting the ball into the pocket.

There is no order in the balls to be dropped into your pocket. Any ball in your pocket is a score as long as there is not a scratch. Three consecutive scratches by a player and the opponent is declared the winner.

First player to have eight balls put into his pocket is the winner.

Safety play is suggested for the player without a shot to score a ball in his pocket. The general rule should be if you can't score a ball try to prevent your opponent from scoring on his next turn.

If player and opponent need only one ball to win and accidentally player drops his winning ball and opponents winning ball in the same shot, the player making his game ball wins.

If player scores a ball in the opponents pocket in error and continues to score in the opponents pocket, opponent must call his attention to the error and player loses his inning at the table but the scored balls count for the opponent.

If all eight balls are scored in error in the opponents pocket, player making the scores wins the game. Opponent must call attention to the error before the winning ball is scored improperly in order to continue in the game.

The game of One Pocket requires skill and practice. It is the masters favorite game and the top professional game. It is one of the most interesting games that can be played, yet beginners should be discouraged from playing it. After a certain degree of proficiency at the table is exhibited in other billiard games, One Pocket should be tried, played and enjoyed.

Eight Ball—Also Known as Solids and Stripes or Black Ball

This game is played with a cue ball and normal rack of fifteen object balls. Balls are racked on the foot spot with the eight ball in the center of the triangle.

The primary purpose of this game is for one player or team to pocket the solid colored group of balls numbered from one to seven or one striped balls from nine to fifteen. Choice of balls to be pocketed is made by first score of player. For example, if the first ball scored in the game is the three ball that player or team must pocket the rest of the balls from one to seven while opposing player or team attempts to pocket all balls from nine to fifteen. Winner of game is the player or team pocketing his numerical group of balls first, following with a legal score on the eight ball.

Player beginning game is determined in the usual manner by lagging. It is not necessary for the beginning player to make a choice on the opening shot nor is it necessary for him to call his shot on the break. When one ball from each group is pocketed on the break that player has his choice of the high or low group. If the player breaking does not pocket a ball on the break his opponent then has his choice of shooting for either the high or low balls.

A player is credited with all balls he legally pockets unless he pockets a ball belonging to his opponent. If this occurs the opponent is credited with that ball. When a player does not pocket one of his balls but pockets an opponents ball it is scored as a miss.

Combination shots are legal at all times except when shooting for the eight ball.

It is required that players shooting for the "high" balls must pocket the fifteen ball in the left side pocket. The player or team scoring the "low" balls must pocket the one ball in the right side pocket. If these balls are pocketed anywhere else they must be spotted and respotted until they are scored in the proper pocket.

After pocketing all balls in their respective numerical groups the players may shoot for the eight ball, calling their shot. On shots other than bank shots the player must pocket the eight ball or cause the eight ball or the cue ball to contact a cushion. Failure to comply with this rule forfeits the game. Game is also forfeited if:

1. A player accidentally pockets the eight ball before pocketing the balls of his numerical group.
2. The player does not contact the eight ball first when playing for that ball.
3. The eight ball is pocketed on a combination.
4. He fails to hit the eight ball on a bank shot.
5. If the eight ball is pocketed in a pocket other than that which was called.
6. If the player shooting for the eight ball scratches the cue ball in a pocket.

If a player has the cue ball in hand and there are object balls within the head string the object ball closest to the string is spotted on the foot spot. This rule also applies when the eight ball is the object ball and lies within the head string.

"9" Ball

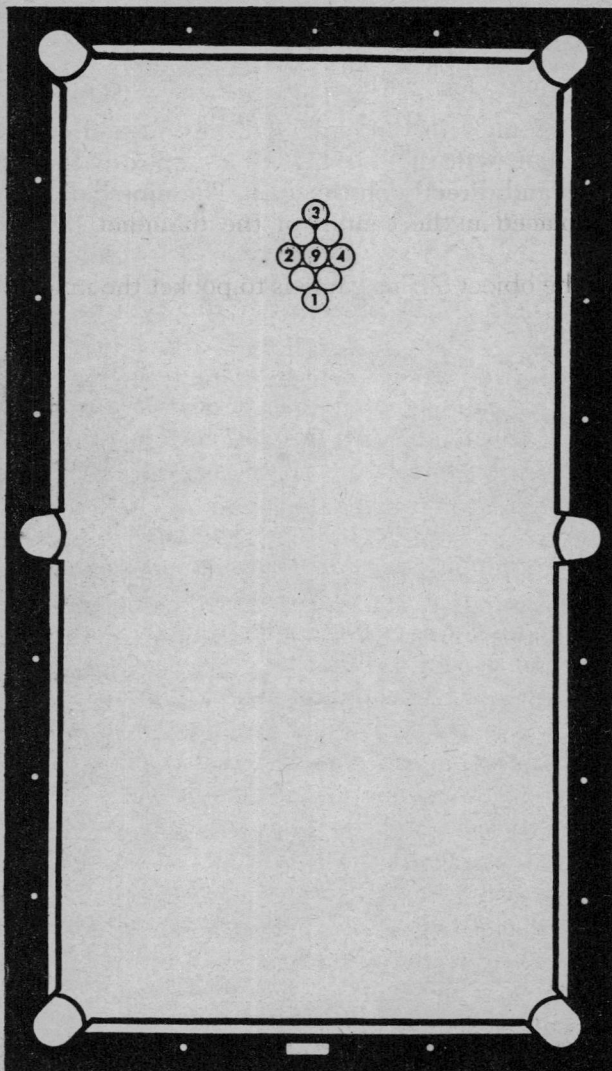

Figure 13

Nine Ball

This game is played with the cue ball and the first nine object balls numbered one through nine. The game requires the use of a special diamond shaped wooden rack for the balls. Balls are racked on the foot spot with the one ball at the apex of the triangle and directly on the spot. The nine ball must be placed in the center of the diamond (Figure 13).

The object of this game is to pocket the nine ball after the first eight have been pocketed legally in rotation.

Player to break is determined in the usual manner by lagging. When, on the break shot where the one ball is hit first any balls pocketed are credited to the shooter. The player must in all successive shots first strike the lowest numbered object ball on the table. The only penalties are loss of turns. Fouls do not cause legally pocketed balls to be forfeited and returned to the table. When it is impossible to hit the lowest numbered ball on the table first the player must attempt to strike the object ball off the cushion, play safe or "shoot out."

The optional "shoot out" rule must be agreed to between players before starting the game. The shoot out option may be exercised when a player does not have a shot. He may with light contact of the cue roll the cue ball to a spot where a shot may possibly be made. The opposing player then must decide whether to take the shot himself or make the first player take the shot. If the first player takes the shot and fails his opponent is then given the cue ball in hand.

The strategy here, with "shoot out," is to set up

a shot that may be too difficult for your opponent but not for yourself. This gives the player an opportunity to take advantage of his or his opponents "Achilles heel."

The loser of a game is given a "break" in succeeding game.

Bank Pool

Bank pool is one of the most challenging games on a six pocket table. Besides requiring skill in bank shots it teaches the value of position play. This game, like "one pocket," is only enjoyable for the player who has acquired a moderate amount of skill at other games.

In "bank pool" the fifteen balls are racked on the foot spot in the usual manner. The player to break is chosen by lagging or the flip of a coin.

The object of this game is to pocket any eight balls before your opponent. Each shot must be a "call" shot except of course on the break.

The top pros when playing "banks," bank every shot. Most players however bank every other shot alternating with straight ins. The first shot after the break is a straight in shot when the alternate rule is in effect. It is permissible to make a bank shot on a straight in turn but a bank must be made on every bank shot turn. To alternate or not should be decided between players before play commences.

The general strategy on the break is to break "safe" leaving your opponent without a shot. A general game plan should include foresight and careful position play while taking full advantage of safety and shoot out rules.

Kiss or combination shots are not allowed in bank pool.

General fouls and penalties apply as in one pocket.

Kelly Pool—Also Known as Pea Pool

There are several games and variations of games that require the use of a shake bottle or "kelly" bottle as it is more popularly known and a set of fifteen numbered pills. Most popular of these games is known as "kelly pool." Kelly, a game for up to seven players, is one of the most exciting and suspenseful games on the table.

In *kelly* the fifteen numbered object balls are racked in the normal fashion on the foot spot. The fifteen numbered pills are shaken in the bottle and two pills are given to each player. Players do not disclose the numbers on the pills drawn.

Play begins by all players disclosing the numerical value of one of their pills. The player showing the lowest numbered pill breaks.

The balls are played in rotation with the object being to be the player to pocket the ball with the same number as the pill being held. If another player legally pockets "your" ball you immediately throw in your pill and are regarded as "killed" and out of competition.

A player is declared the winner when he either legally pockets "his" ball or legally "kills" the last player in competition with him.

Some of the most important strategy comes into play when the pills are disclosed for the break. For instance, if you have the twelve and fifteen pill and

31

there are four average players in the game you would want to throw your fifteen pill and so as to let everyone else shoot first. Hopefully when your turn came up you would only have to run three or four balls to win instead of running twelve balls.

General rules and penalties apply in *kelly*.

"Bottle-Pool"

The requirements for this game are one and two numbered object balls, the cue ball and a "kelly" bottle. The primary object of this game is to score exactly 31 points before your opponent. If however a player scores more than 31 points his inning is ended and his score is reduced to only the points scored in excess of 31. For instance if a player inadvertently scores 34 points his inning is ended and his score becomes 3 or the difference between 31 and 34.

Scores are made in the following manner:

A. One point is scored for a carom on two object balls.
B. One point is scored for pocketing the one ball.
C. Two points is scored for pocketing the two ball.
D. Five points is scored for a carom from object ball which upsets the shake bottle. It is possible to score in each manner on one stroke for nine points.

If a carom from an object ball flips the shake bottle upright on its base the game is automatically won by the player accomplishing this feat.

The player reaching exactly thirty-one points

Bottle Pool

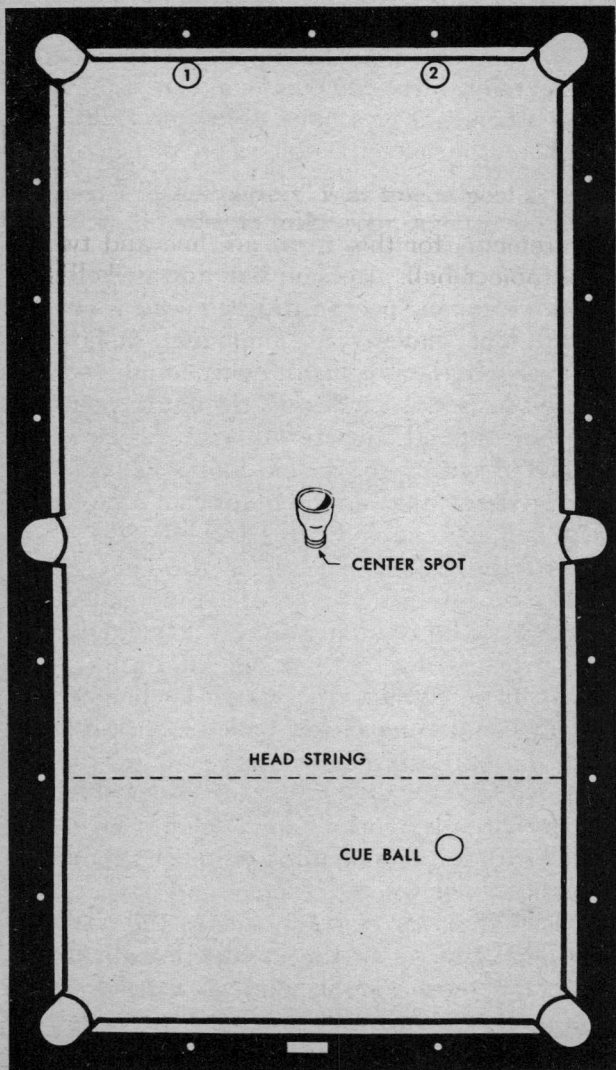

Figure 14

must announce this fact before his opponent shoots. If this is not done his victory may not be acknowledged until his next regular inning. If however in the meantime his opponent reaches the exact score of thirty-one points and announces this fact he becomes the winner.

To begin the game the objects are placed in their respective positions. (Figure 14.) The one ball at the left diamond on the foot cushion. The two balls placed at the right diamond on the foot cushion. The shake bottle is placed upside down on its open end on the center spot. Starting player has cue ball in hand. The players (no limit) determine rotation of play by lagging or drawing numbered pills from the kelly bottle. Players do not have to call their shot but must make either of the two balls their first object.

If the designated spot at the foot rail for an object ball is occupied after that ball has been pocketed the ball is spotted on the center spot. Should the center spot be occupied the ball should be placed at the head spot. The bottle never may be the primary object of the cue ball until the one ball has made contact with an object ball. A shot does not count if an object ball strikes the bottle before the bottle has been contacted by the cue ball.

When bottle is knocked down it must be placed upright with the open end down on the spot or as close to the spot where the open end of the bottle lay when the bottle came to rest. The player loses his turn if he forces the bottle into a pocket or off the table. Should this happen it is spotted on the center spot.

A player's inning is ended if he commits a foul. The points scored on the foul stroke are not allowed and the player is penalized one additional point. The following situations are fouls:

A. Failure to hit object ball on a strike.
B. Upsetting of bottle by object ball, cue, clothing, etc.
C. Forcing of the cue ball into the pocket or off the table.
D. Upsetting a bottle by cue ball without striking an object ball.
E. Shooting without one foot on the floor.

"41"

"41" requires the fifteen object balls be racked in a normal fashion on the foot spot. A "kelly" bottle and pills numbered one to fifteen are also needed for this game. Rotation of play is determined by each player drawing a pill from the bottle. The player with the lowest number must break. Other players follow with lowest number first.

Before actual start of play players draw another pill from the bottle which the number of which is not disclosed.

The object of this game is to score enough points to total 41 when added to the number on the pill being held by the player. Point values correspond to the numerical value of the object ball pocketed.

An inning consists of one shot only whether or not a ball is pocketed. A player is declared winner when he attains a score of 41 including the numerical value of his pill. The game is also over when all of the balls are pocketed without a player reaching 41. Should this happen the player closest in score to 41 is the winner.

A scratch is called when a player misses or pockets the cue ball. On a scratch the player must give up any balls that may have been pocketed on that shot plus one additional ball as a penalty. If he has legally scored more than one ball he may spot the ball of his choice. If however a player owes the table a ball and has none to his credit he must spot the first ball he scores should he owe the table a ball and pocket more than one ball on a shot he may spot the ball of his choice.

A player scoring over 41 points has "burst" and must spot all of the balls he has scored. The last ball scored must be placed on or as close to as possible the foot spot.

A new number may be drawn by a player who bursts if he chooses.

Safety play in forty-one demands that the cue ball be driven to a rail before or after contacting the object ball. A scratch is called if this is not done and the guilty player owes a ball to the table.

A player who "bursts" without declaring so is disqualified from further play in that game.

Fifteen Ball

For this game the fifteen numbered balls are racked in a triangle on the foot spot. The fifteen ball is placed at the apex of the triangle on the foot spot with the next highest balls in value placed behind the fifteen ball and all lower numbered balls to the rear of the rack.

Breaking player is determined in the usual fashion. Player to break starts with cue ball in hand. On the break shot it is required that a ball is pocketed or at least two object balls driven to a cushion. A call is not necessary on the break.

The object in "fifteen ball" is to score 61 points first. The numerical value of each ball pocketed by a player is credited to his point total. For instance, if on the break the player pocketed the six ball his point total at that point would be six points. Every time a shot is taken by a player a ball must be pocketed or an object ball must be driven to a rail or the cue ball must be made to carom off of an object ball into a cushion. Player receives credit for all balls pocketed on a single stroke. Call shots are not necessary in this game.

A three point penalty is levied against a player for the following reasons:

1. If the player fails to pocket a ball or drive two object balls to a cushion on the break. He also is required if his opponent chooses, to rerack the balls and break again with a three point penalty assessed for each succeeding failure.
2. If a player scratches on the cue ball.
3. If a player during the course of play does not pocket an object ball or drive one to a cushion or if the cue ball does not contact the cushion after hitting an object ball.
4. If a player forces the cue ball off of the table.
5. Shooting out of turn. If this error is not detected by the opponent and a score is made the player continues shooting.
6. Interference with the cue ball after a shot.
7. Shooting while a ball is in motion.
8. Failure to have at least one foot on the floor while shooting.

If a player commits more than one foul on same stroke he is penalized for one foul only and loses only three points.

In case of a tie the players may spot the fifteen ball, lag for the first shot and open play with the cue ball in hand behind the head string. The player scoring the fifteen ball first wins.

Rotation

A cue ball and fifteen object balls are used in rotation. The object balls are racked in the triangle on the foot spot with the one ball on the foot spot, and two in the left triangle apex and the three ball in the right triangle apex.

The order of play is determined and player designated to break starts with cue ball in hand. It is compulsory that the one ball be the first object ball. Failure to contact the one ball on the break shot is an error and ends that players inning. Any balls pocketed on this illegal stroke are spotted. The next player accepts balls in position and continues with the one ball as the object. The winner of this game is that player or team scoring 61 points first. Object balls must be in numerical order and be first ball contacted on each stroke. Failure is an error and ends that players inning. Balls other than the object ball which are pocketed after legal contact with the object ball are credited to the players score. At all times the object ball must be the lowest numbered ball on the table. A cue ball scratch ends the players inning and balls pocketed on the scratch shot are spotted.

Balls to be spotted are placed on the long string running from the foot spot to the center diamond of the foot rail. Balls must be spotted in numerical order with the lowest numbered ball directly on the foot spot and all successive balls frozen in order behind it on the string. An object ball or cue ball resting on the long string is never moved to make room for spotting a ball. In this case balls to be spotted are placed either in front or behind these interfering balls. If the entire string between the foot spot and foot rail should become filled up balls to be spotted should be placed in front of the foot spot as close as possible to the spot.

An object ball is spotted if it jumps the table. If player on a legal shot pockets a ball but also causes one or more object balls to jump the table he may continue to play after spotting the jumped balls and is credited with the balls he pocketed on that stroke. If no score was made his inning is ended. It is an error at anytime if the cue ball jumps the table and the inning is ended. Balls pocketed on that stroke are spotted and opponent steps to the table with cue ball in hand.

14.1 Continuous

This is the game that for years has been used to decide champions in all major tournaments. Recent years have seen games like one pocket and nine ball edge into the top competitions, however 14.1 is still "the" game.

14.1 like most pool games is best for individual against individual but can also be played with partners or teams. Play begins with the fifteen object balls racked on the foot spot with the fifteen ball in the apex of the triangle on the foot spot itself. The one ball is placed in the left apex of the triangle and the five ball placed in the right apex. The rest of the higher numbered balls should be placed near the rear of the rack.

Winner of lag for break usually assigns the break to his opponent because of the improbability of a legal score on the break shot. Breaking player has cue ball in hand and must drive two or more object balls to a cushion or pocket an object ball. If a ball is pocketed credit is not given unless that shot was called. If rules for the break are not followed by the starting player the shot is considered a foul and that player loses two points. The opposing player also may choose whether the player committing the foul should lose his inning or rerack the balls and break again. A two point penalty is assessed for each successive failure in meeting break requirements.

If, on the break, the opening player scratches the cue ball but drives two object balls to a cushion he loses his inning and is assessed a one point penalty. Incoming player then starts with cue ball in hand.

On the break shot the player may shoot directly at the "rack" in the normal fashion or direct the cue ball off of one or more cushions before contacting the balls.

The incoming player accepts balls in position when opening player is scoreless on his break shot.

In tournament play the winner is the player scoring 150 points first. At times a lower number of points may be agreed upon by the contestants.

In tournament play the title often depends on more than one "block" of points. Each block of points to be a number agreed upon in advance by the contestants. For instance, if the agreed on block score is 125 the winner is the player scoring 125 points first. He must however continue to shoot until he pockets all of the object balls on the table but one. If a player wins a block by scoring the necessary number of points but misses in his attempt to clear the table of all the remaining object balls but one, the opponent may come to the table for a chance to clear all of the object balls but one and make the opening break shot in the next block.

In successive blocks the contestant scoring the agreed on number of points first wins the block. If the winner of the second block is behind in total points for the match, play must continue until one of the players has scored his total of 250 points or the number required for two blocks. If this situation occurs in succeeding blocks, play must continue until one player has scored 375 points or multiples of the agreed on score.

All shots in the game of 14.1 continuous must be "called." The player must clearly indicate to the referee what ball he intends to pocket and the pocket in which he expects to score. Combination, carom and bank shots are legal in 14.1 continuous. The player is credited with one point for every ball legally pocketed. If on a legal stroke, other balls are pocketed besides the one called, he is credited with one point for each extra ball. Object balls illegally pocketed should be spotted on the long string as in rotation.

A player must on each shot make a legitimate try to pocket an object ball. Failure to do so ends his inning with no penalty providing that the cue ball hits at least one other object ball driving it into a cushion or pocket or providing that the cue ball

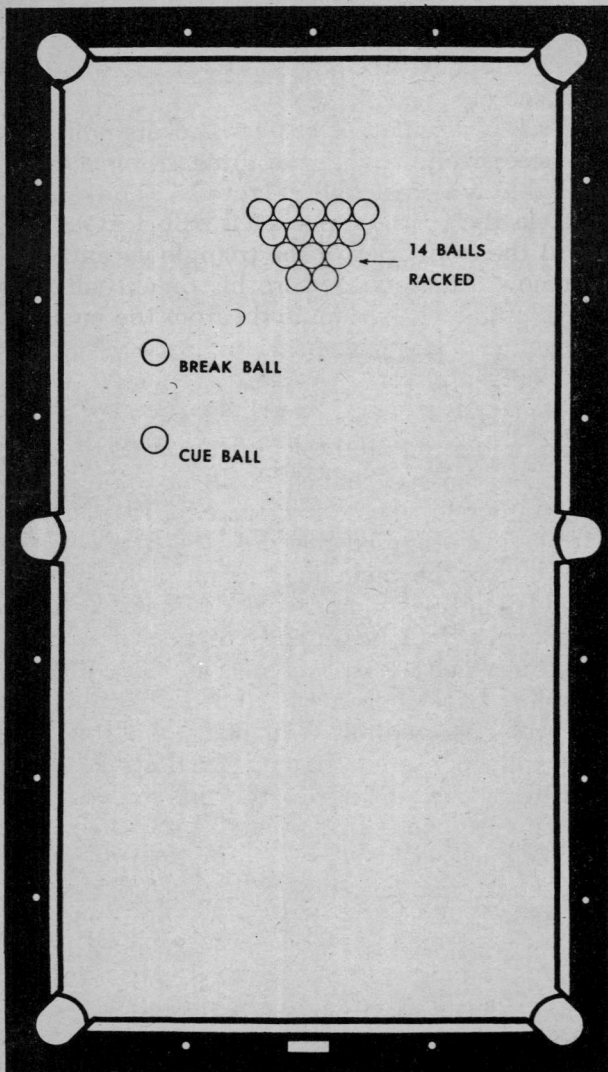

14 BALLS
RACKED

BREAK BALL

CUE BALL

Figure 15

hits a cushion after hitting an object ball. If the player fails to do this it is considered a foul and ends the inning with the loss of one point from that players score.

In 14.1 continuous a player pockets fourteen balls successively leaving the fifteenth object ball on the table as a break ball. (Figure 15.) The referee then racks the fourteen pocketed balls leaving the space at the front apex of the triangle vacant. The player now attempts to score his break ball in a pocket designated by him and carom the cue ball off of the break ball into the triangle of racked balls with enough force to "break" the rack.

The player continues play if he pockets the break ball or calls and pockets a shot in the rack. Player continues shooting fourteen balls at a time having them reracked and breaking until he misses, scratches or scores the required number of points.

A player commits a foul and is forfeited one point if he stops the cue ball in front of an object ball that is frozen against a cushion even though he contacts the object ball. When playing a shot of this type (as a "safety") the player must either pocket the object ball or cause the cue ball to contact a cushion after striking the object ball or force the object ball to another cushion.

In a situation of the above type each player will be allowed but two shots on this safety. On the third shot the player must drive the object ball to a different cushion or drive the cue ball to any other cushion after contact with the object ball. If this is not done the referee must rack all fifteen balls and with cue ball in hand the offending player must break according to the opening rules of the game. If a player using the safety procedure noted above commits three scratches before the two shot limit or as a result of his two shots in the safety procedure he is penalized one point for each scratch and fifteen points for three consecutive scratches.

When player with cue ball in hand shoots after having been warned by the referee that his cue ball is not behind the head string he loses his inning and forfeits one point. The opposing player then may accept the balls as they lay or elect that conditions be restored to what they were before the foul was committed. If the cue ball is not within the head string and player shoots before the foul is noticed he is credited for any score made on that shot. If he misses it merely ends his inning.

A one point penalty is assessed a player when the following fouls are committed:

1. Player must have one foot on the floor when shooting.
2. Player must not in any manner disturb or touch the cue ball or an object ball with any foreign object including the side with his cue, clothing or part of his body.
3. A player must not take a stroke while a cue ball or object ball is moving or spinning. When this foul is committed the incoming player may insist that the balls be returned to the condition prior to the foul or accept the balls in current position. Referee is to be the sole judge in restoring balls to position.

Safety play is legal in 14.1 continuous. It is not necessary for a player to declare his intention to play safe, however, when an obvious safety has been played, the referee should announce "safety" when the balls stop rolling. In playing a safety the player must drive the object ball to a cushion, pocket an object ball or cause the cue ball to strike a rail after contacting an object ball. Failure is a foul with a penalty of one point.

The fifteen point penalty rule: When a player has scratched he is penalized one point and a notation is made that he has one scratch against him. On his next turn at the table the offending player may remove this scratch by either pocketing a ball or by playing a legal safety. If he scratches during this appearance at the table with one scratch against him he of course loses his inning, forfeits one more point and the notation is made by the referee that he now has two scratches against him. At his next turn at the table the offending player may remove both scratches by either pocketing a ball, playing a legal safety or obviously trying to pocket a called ball. If however he scratches for a third time in succession he suffers the loss of one point for the third scratch plus an extra fifteen point penalty for three successive scratches. He is then required to take cue ball in hand and break the fifteen balls with the opening break shot rules applying.

If the referee is of the opinion that a player has purposely moved the cue ball for a safety with anything but the tip of the cue or has purposely committed a foul he will be penalized fifteen points with the incoming player accepting balls in position.

If an object ball rebounds back to the table after being in a pocket it cannot be considered a pocketed ball. The player loses his inning and the ball remains in play where it comes to rest on the table.

When a player forces the cue ball to jump from the table it is considered a foul with the player losing the inning and one point. A scratch is also marked against him. Opposing player starts play with cue ball in hand. When in the case of a called ball jumping a table it is considered a miss and the players inning is ended. Retrieved object ball is then spotted. If a called ball is pocketed but another ball, as a result of the stroke jumps the table, it is retrieved, spotted with the player receiving credit for the legally pocketed ball and continuing play.

A lighting fixture placed directly over the table is considered part of the equipment. If a ball should jump the table and strike the lighting fixtures and return to the table surface it may remain in play where it comes to rest with no penalty applied.

If a ball jumps the table and rides a rail returning to the table it remains in play where it comes to rest. This is not to be considered a jumped ball.

If a ball leaves the table coming to rest on a rail without returning to the table surface it is to be considered a jumped ball with the proper rule applying depending on whether the ball is the cue ball or an object ball.

A jump shot is a legal play when the player causes the ball to rise from the bed of the table accidentally as the result of a legal stroke or on purpose by elevating the butt of the cue in striking the cue ball in a manner causing it to "jump." A jump shot however is not permissible when the player digs under the cue ball with the end of his cue. The referee shall decide if a foul has been committed and if so the offending player suffers the loss of one point.

When cue ball is in hand and all object balls on the table are behind the head string the referee must spot the object ball closest to the string on the foot spot. When two balls are of equal distance from the string the lowest numbered ball is chosen to be spotted.

The cue ball shall be "in hand" at the beginning of the game, when forced off the table or pocketed, and when for any reason fifteen balls are racked. (Except when superceded by certain interference rulings.) The cue ball remains in hand until driven by the player from behind the head string to any point on the table between the head string and the foot. Whenever a player pockets the fourteenth and fifteenth balls of a frame (whether inadvertently or not) he is credited for both balls and play is resumed with the fifteen object balls reracked and the player shooting from where the cue ball came to rest.

In a situation where the "break" ball (the unpocketed fifteenth ball of the frame) interferes with reracking the fourteen balls the break ball shall be placed on the head spot. Should both the cue ball and break ball interfere with racking of the fourteen balls the correct procedure would be to rack all fifteen object balls in the normal fashion on the foot spot and play would continue with cue ball in hand.

The following rulings apply when the cue ball interferes with racking of the fourteen object balls.

A. Player gets cue ball in hand if the break ball

is in front of the head string (between head string and foot of table).

B. Cue ball is placed on head spot when break ball is behind head string. Should the ball be resting on the head spot the cue ball is placed on the center spot.

In all cases of interference with racking the fourteen balls the player has the choice of shooting at the break ball if it has not been racked or any ball in the rack. If player chooses to shoot into the rack of fourteen balls he must cause an object ball to strike a cushion, or drive a cue ball to a cushion after hitting an object ball or legally pocket a ball. Should this not be accomplished the player is penalized one point.

Should a ball or balls be disturbed on purpose or by accident by persons other than players involved the balls should be replaced as close to their original position as possible. Player then continues his inning.

Competing players must lodge foul protests with referee before player allegedly committing foul shoots again. Protests will not be honored by the referee if this rule is not complied with.

"Line-Up"

This game requires the cue ball and fifteen object balls. Object balls are racked on the foot spot in a normal fashion with starting player having cue ball in hand. Every shot in this game must be a called shot. Each player is credited with one point for every ball legally pocketed. Winner of game is that player who first scores the agreed on number of points. This game is usually played for at least 25 points.

A two point penalty is assessed if the starting player does not pocket a called ball in the rack or drive two object balls to a cushion. Opposing player can insist that starting player repeat his "break shot" until fulfilling the break shot requirements. A two point penalty is opposed for each succeeding failure. At the conclusion of each inning the player records his points scored. He then spots all of the balls pocketed on the long string line. If a player scores all fifteen balls they are respotted on the long string line. The player then continues shooting with cue ball from where it came to rest after previous shot.

General rules for 14.1 continuous apply in line-up.

"Cowboy"

This game combines the respective skills and demands of carom and pocket billiards. It is played with the cue ball and the one, three and five object balls.

The object balls are placed as follows: three ball on the foot spot; five ball on the center spot with the one ball on the head spot. The starting player with cue ball in hand must begin play from behind the head string with the three ball as the first object ball.

The object of this game is to score exactly 101 points. The scoring must be done in three segments. One of 90 points, one of 10 points and one of 1 point. The first 90 points must be scored using the following point values:

A. One point scored for a carom on two object balls.

B. Two points scored for a carom on three object balls.

C. Face value scored for pocketing an object ball. For instance the three ball if legally pocketed gives the player three points.

After each player attains the score of 90 points exactly he must make the next ten points by carom scores only. After scoring 100 points the last point is scored by a carom shot of the cue ball off of the one ball into a pocket "called" by the player. The cue ball must not contact a second object ball before the cue ball goes into the pocket. If the cue ball is pocketed in a pocket not called the player loses all points scored in an inning if he fouls.

Special rules:

A. An object ball when pocketed must be placed on its original spot.

B. Should the original spot be occupied the ball or balls to be spotted must be held off of the table until spots become open.

C. If a player with exactly 100 points is at the table and the one ball is pocketed he may have the balls spotted as in the beginning of the game and commence play with the cue ball in hand from behind the head string.

D. A player with exactly ninety points loses his turn and points scored in that inning if he pockets an object ball while scoring from ninety-one to a hundred.

E. Except for the hundred and first point the

Golf Pool

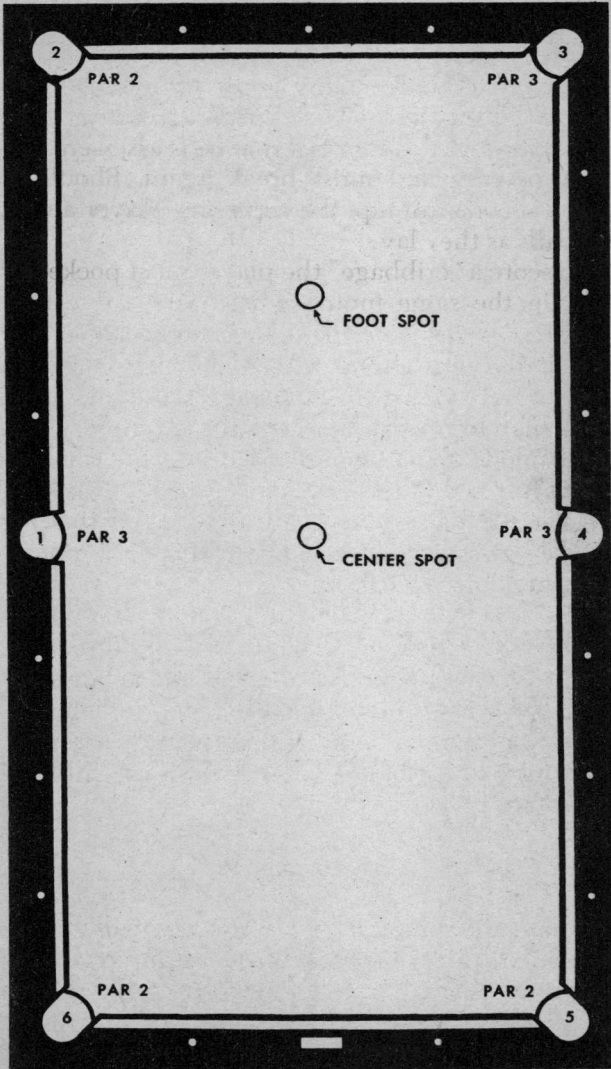

Figure 16

Rotation of play is determined by lagging. To begin play the cue ball is placed on the center spot with the object ball on the foot spot.

The starting player must attempt to bank the object ball off the foot cushion on the first stroke into "hole number one." (Figure 16.) Should he miss he continues to shoot until he pockets the ball. All succeeding shots may be banks or straight ins as the player chooses. When the ball is pocketed the number of strokes taken become the players score for the first "hole." The next player at the table starts with the balls in the same position with the cue ball in the center spot and the object ball on the foot spot. He also must attempt a bank shot from the fool rail on his first stroke trying to score the ball in "hole number one." If he misses he continues shooting till the ball is scored and his number of strokes are noted for his score on the first.

On each succeeding hole the players start by spotting the object ball on the foot spot with the cue ball left where it came to rest after the previous player scored his hole. Players on succeeding holes are not required to bank any shot. Each player continues to shoot until the ball is pocketed in the proper hole and his number of strokes are recorded and added to his score. The player completing the six holes in the fewest number of strokes is the game winner.

General rules:

A. After the first "hole" the cue ball is always played from where it came to rest after the preceding stroke.

B. A player commits a scratch when he pockets the cue ball or object ball in the wrong pocket.

Penalty for a scratch is four points. Scratched balls are spotted and the player continues shooting till his "hole" is made legally.

C.   The player must on every shot either pocket the object ball in the proper pocket, or cause the object ball to touch a cushion or cause the cue ball to touch a cushion after hitting the object ball. If this is not done the player is guilty of foul and four strokes are added to his score. Player continues shooting till his hole is made legally.

D.   If cue ball is spotted and object ball lies within the head string the player shoots at the object ball in that position.

"Mr. and Mrs."

This game is devised to encourage women to play as it tends to equalize the skill of the players. The game combines aspects of rotation and basic pocket billiards.

This game is played with the normal rack of fifteen object balls and the cue ball. Object balls are racked on the foot spot as in rotation. Rotation of play is determined by lagging and the starting player has cue ball in hand.

The main object of this game is for a player or team to score 61 points before the opposition. Points are scored according to the face value of the ball pocketed.

Player must on the break make the one ball on the foot spot his first object ball. That player or team is credited with all balls scored on the break if the one ball is contacted first by the cue ball.

On succeeding play the men are required to

play all balls in rotation and make the object balls in numerical order. Women players may attempt to score the ball of their choice. Players are not required to call their shots and all balls pocketed on combination or kiss shots are legal except that the man must always hit the lowest ball on the table first.

Should a man pocket an object ball not in rotation his inning is ended and the ball is spotted. If any player scratches the cue ball his inning is ended and the object balls if any pocketed on that stroke are also spotted. Balls should be spotted in numerical order as in rotation from the foot spot back towards the foot rail.

Should an incoming player with cue ball in hand as the result of a previous players scratch be required to hit the low ball behind the head string the low ball must be spotted on the foot spot.

One and Nine ball

"One and nine ball" is a game for four players. Rotation of play is determined by lagging. It is played with the normal rack of fifteen object balls and a cue ball. The general rules of 14.1 continuous and rotation apply. Balls are racked as in rotation.

The object of this game is for two partners to score 61 points before the other team.

Partners are determined in the fashion: Player scoring the one ball automatically is the partner of the player scoring the nine ball. Should the same player score the one and nine ball he becomes the partner of the player who pockets the next possible ball, the ten ball. All balls must be pocketed in rotation.

56

In case of a tie where all balls are pocketed and each side has 60 points the player pocketing the last ball places that ball on the foot spot and shoots with cue ball in hand behind the head string. Play continues until one side pockets that ball.

"Baseball"

This game is played with the cue ball and twenty-one object balls numbered one through twenty-one which require a special triangle with a twenty-one ball capacity. The balls are racked on the foot spot in the normal fashion. In this game the foot spot is called "home plate." The nine ball is called the "pitcher."

Rotation of play is determined by lagging with starting player having cue ball in hand. The object of this game is to score the most "runs." Runs correspond with face value of all balls legally pocketed by a player.

Each player has nine innings which are played in succession without alternating innings with the other players. An inning is ended when a player misses or loses his turn as the result of a foul.

After the opening break shot the players must call their shots, ball and pocket. When a player pockets a ball and scratches, the object ball involved must be spotted on the "home plate." Upon a scratch the players inning is ended. Scores are posted by inning on a score sheet. Scratches are also penalized by forefeiture of the last ball legally pocketed. Should a player be scoreless in the game at that point he spots the next ball legally scored. If a player does not pocket the called ball but pockets other balls the illegally pocketed balls are spotted and the inning is ended. If a player runs all the balls before his nine innings are completed the balls are reracked and the player continues until nine innings are completed.

"Poker"

This game requires the white cue ball, a special set of sixteen object balls and a special diamond shaped rack with a sixteen ball capacity. The entire rack of sixteen balls is set up on the foot spot of the table.

The object of this game is to score balls whose face value make the best poker hand as in cards. The balls are marked as follows. Aces—4. Kings—4. Queens—4. Jacks—4. Fifteen of the balls are numbered one through fifteen while the sixteenth, a Jack is only marked "J" on both sides.

Rotation of play is determined by lag with the starting player having cue ball in hand. Starting player is credited with all balls pocketed on the break providing that no foul is committed. If he scores he continues shooting till a miss, a foul or he pockets five balls. At no time is a player allowed to pocket more than five balls in one inning. Incoming players accepts balls in position. This game is good for two to four players.

The game is over when all balls have been pocketed legally. For example, one player may have five balls to his credit, another may have two balls to his credit, still a third may have four balls in his hand while a fourth player has three balls in his hand. In this case two object balls remain on the table. The player having already scored five balls may continue to shoot in turn in effect to improve his hand. Each time he pockets a ball he must spot the ball of his choice from his hand. He may continue to pocket and respot balls in effort to strengthen his hand until he misses or scores the limit of five balls per inning. A player with four balls in his hand may pocket the fifth ball and continue to shoot for the last ball in effort to strengthen his hand. A player with two or three balls to their credit will end the game if they pocket the two balls on the table.

When all balls are pocketed the players then "lay down their hand" with the best hand winning. A player who has not scored five balls is not necessarily a loser. For instance if he has three balls, all queens, he would win over the player who has five balls but whose best "hand" may only be three jacks or two pair. If a player has only one ball to his credit he defeats a player with no balls at all.

There will be times when a player with five balls in his hand cannot strengthen his hand by pocketing any ball on the table. In a case like this he will miss deliberately rather than pocket a ball that will weaken his hand. In making a deliberate miss the player must drive an object ball to a rail or cause the cue ball to carom off an object ball into a rail. Failure of this rule is a foul. Each foul is a penalty of one ball. A player may choose the ball to carom off an object ball into a rail. Failure of this rule is a foul. Each foul is a penalty of one ball. A player may choose the ball from his hand to be spotted. The following situations are fouls:

A. Failure to hit an object ball.
B. Pocketing the cue ball.
C. Forcing the cue ball off the table.

D. Shooting without one foot on the floor.

E. Touching the cue ball with anything except the tip of the cue on a stroke or touches on an object ball in play on the table except by contact of the cue ball.

F. Failure to comply with the previously noted rule on deliberate misses.

Players if they choose may agree to use the balls marked with a J as "wild cards."

"American Snooker"

The game of snooker requires a special set of twenty-one object balls and a white cue ball. The game is usually played on a specially constructed 5x10 or 6x12 foot pool table. (Figures 17 and 18.) It is also possible to play this game on 4x8 and 4½x9 foot pool tables.

Fifteen of the object balls are colored red with a scoring value of one point each. The other six object balls are different colors and have different values as follows: Yellow—2 points. Green—3 points. Brown—4 points. Blue—5 points. Pink—6 points. Black—7 points. Highest score at games end determines the winner. The game is ended when all balls are off the table. The winning score is not decisive since points and additional penalties enter into the final score factor.

The balls are racked for the games beginning as indicated in diagram Number Nine.

Start of play is determined by lag with starting player having cue ball in hand. In snooker this means that the ball may be put into play from anywhere within the "D." (Figures 17-18.) On the

American Snooker
(6 x 12 Ft. Table)

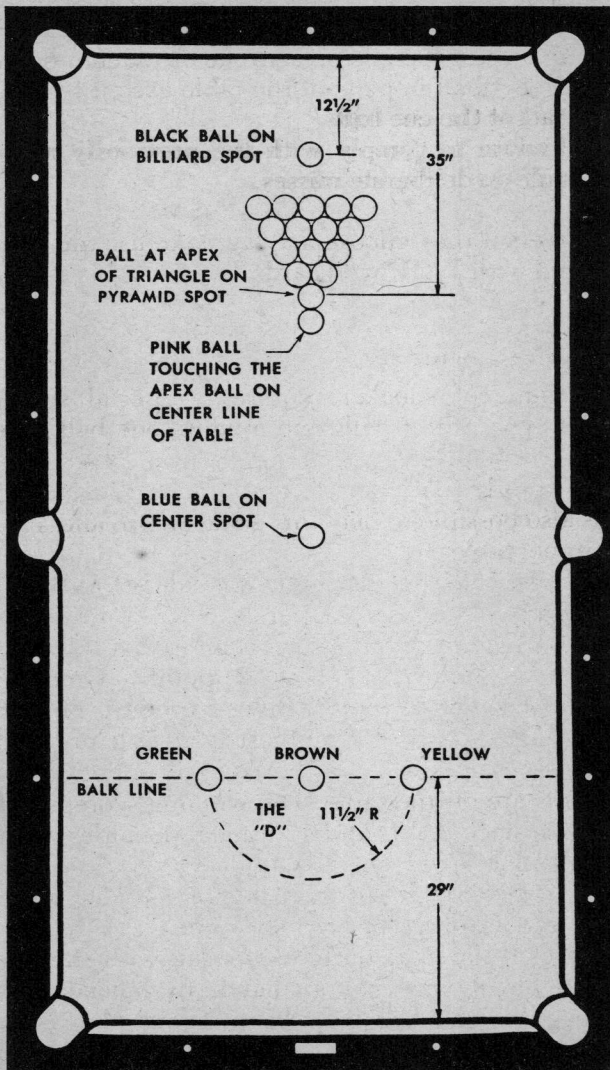

12½"

BLACK BALL ON
BILLIARD SPOT

35"

BALL AT APEX
OF TRIANGLE ON
PYRAMID SPOT

PINK BALL
TOUCHING THE
APEX BALL ON
CENTER LINE
OF TABLE

BLUE BALL ON
CENTER SPOT

GREEN   BROWN   YELLOW

BALK LINE

THE
"D"   11½" R

29"

Figure 17

American Snooker
(5 x 10-Ft. Table)

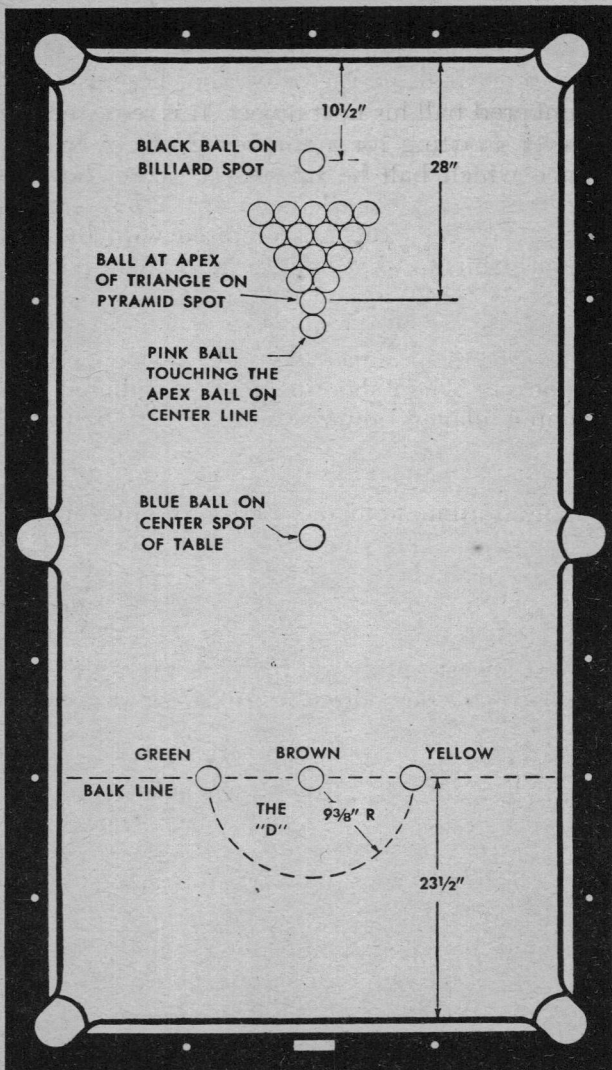

10½"

BLACK BALL ON
BILLIARD SPOT

28"

BALL AT APEX
OF TRIANGLE ON
PYRAMID SPOT

PINK BALL
TOUCHING THE
APEX BALL ON
CENTER LINE

BLUE BALL ON
CENTER SPOT
OF TABLE

GREEN   BROWN   YELLOW

BALK LINE

THE   9⅜" R
"D"

23½"

Figure 18

break shot the player must contact a red ball first. He is entitled to credit for any or all of the red balls made on the break shot. If the player scores one or more balls on the break shot he must make a numbered ball his next object. It is required that a player shooting for a numbered object ball announce which ball he intends to score, however it is not necessary to call the pocket. When a player scores an object ball he is credited with the face value of points for that ball. In subsequent play the player must alternate red balls and numbered balls in his scoring. Call shots are not necessary on the red balls, however he must always call the ball (not the pocket) when shooting for a numbered ball. Incoming players always make a red ball their first object.

Numbered balls after having been scored are to be spotted up immediately before the player takes his next shot. This rule does not apply when all red balls have been pocketed. If, however, the numbered balls proper spot is occupied by another ball, the ball to be spotted is placed on the spot of the next lowest numbered ball. For example, if the pink ball is to be spotted and its spot is occupied the pink ball should be spotted on the blue balls spot. Scoring is recorded at the end of each inning. Scoring is recorded at the end of each inning.

After all red balls are off the table the players continue to pocket the numbered balls in rotation. At this time the numbered balls remain in the pockets as they are legally scored.

Forcing the cue ball off of the table is a foul and ends the inning of the offending player. Any balls scored on a foul stroke are spotted unless they are red in which case they remain in the pocket with no score credit. Incoming player has cue ball in hand within the "D." Numbered object balls scored on a foul stroke are spotted. If a red ball is pocketed as a result of a shot where the cue ball jumps the table, the red ball remains in the pocket. In any case the player cannot receive any points on a foul stroke. Should a numbered ball be forced off of the table it would be respotted. If a player scored a red ball and as the result of that shot caused a numbered ball to jump the table the numbered ball would be spotted with the player continuing his inning with credit for one red ball scored. If player shooting for a numbered ball scores that ball and causes another numbered ball to jump the table on the same stroke both numbered balls are spotted with the player continuing his inning with score for the called numbered ball. If a player forces the object ball off the table without scoring his inning is over with no penalty. If the player scores a red ball and forces another red ball off the table in the same stroke he receives credit for one red ball scored with both red balls remaining off the the table. In a case where a ball is forced off the table and hits a light fixture directly above the table and returns to the table it is put into play where it comes to rest.

In snooker when the player has the cue ball in hand (within the "D") he may shoot at any ball on the table even if it is not in front of the head string. In other words he does not have to spot his object ball if it is behind the head string.

If a player after scoring a numbered ball does not make sure that his numbered ball is spotted properly before he shoots again and his opponent calls this error it is a foul with the player losing his inning. If his opponent does not detect the error he continues play. If he shoots and misses he loses his inning with no penalty.

Two balls may not be pocketed on the same stroke unless they are red balls. Two balls may not be struck simultaneously unless they are red balls. It is counted a foul if the player when pocketing a red ball legally pockets a numbered ball on the same stroke. A score may not be counted as a result of that stroke and the player loses his inning and the penalty. The red ball in this case remains in the pocket with the numbered ball placed on its proper spot. This same ruling applies if a player pockets a numbered ball other than the called numbered ball. If a player strikes two balls simultaneously other than two reds he ends his inning with no penalty.

When the cue ball is touching another ball the player may shoot at the ball the cue ball is touching or may shoot at any other legal object ball. If he elects to play a safety on the touching ball he must make sure to drive the touching ball to a cushion or cause the cue ball to hit a cushion after moving the touching ball.

"Snookered" is the term that applies to a player who cannot shoot in a straight line at a ball that he is on because of interference of other balls on the table. When a player is "snookered" he still must first hit the ball he is on using bank shots if necessary. It is a foul to contact first a ball that you are not on. If a "snookered" player fails to hit any ball on the table he has fouled.

If a player seeking to pocket the numbered object balls in rotation after all of the reds are off the table fails to hit first the ball he is on or fails to hit any ball at all he has fouled.

Additional fouls are as follows:

A. Touching the cue ball more than once with the tip of the cue on any one stroke.
B. A cue ball scratch in the pocket.
C. Jumping a cue ball off of the table.
D. Shooting without at least one foot on the floor.
E. Shooting before all balls on the table have stopped motion.
F. Playing with an improper ball.
G. Shooting before balls have been spotted.
H. Playing when balls are improperly spotted as previously discussed.
I. Contacting a cue or object ball except on a legal stroke.
J. Interference on a moving ball.
K. Playing improperly when cue ball is in hand.
L. Playing out of turn.
M. Making a miss.
N. Pocketing two numbered object balls on the same stroke.

After a foul has been committed the incoming player has the choice of refusing the next shot whether he is snookered or not. Should he refuse the shot the opponent must shoot again. On each successive foul the player is penalized seven points and the incoming player retains the option of taking or refusing the next shot. An inning is not complete until a legal shot has been made or the incoming player elects to take the shot.

Safety plays are legal in snooker. In a safety the player must drive his object ball to a cushion or cause the cue ball to carom into a cushion after hitting the object ball.

Push shots are legal if the cue does not strike the cue ball more than once.

A player not trying to strike the ball shall forfeit seven points. Failure to make a legal shot on a following turn shall cost the offending player an additional seven points with his opponent having the choice of accepting the shot that lies or insisting his opponent play until he executes a legal shot.

A foul must be claimed by the opposing player or announced by the referee before the guilty player makes a subsequent stroke. When a foul is claimed and proven the offending player may not score, he loses his turn, he loses his right to snooker his opponent and he forefeits points as per the rule.

Penalties for fouls are exercised by forfeitures. This means that instead of subtracting penalty points from a player the number of points is added to the opponents score. For example if a player commits a foul the penalty of seven points is added on to his opponent. All fouls have a forfeiture value of seven points.

Bumper Pool

Bumper pool is played by two players or by four as partners. Each side has five red balls or five white balls, one of each color being a marked cue ball.

To set up bumper pool, place two red balls on each side of white cup on markers, placing marked red ball directly in front of white cup. Place white balls in same position around the red cup.

Both players shoot marked ball at the same time,

hitting first the side-cushion, banking the ball into or near his color cup. The player who plays his ball into or nearest to his cup shoots again. Marked cue balls must be pocketed first. If a player sinks another ball before his marked ball is pocketed, his opponent may remove two of his own balls and drop them into his cup. In the event that both marked balls are pocketed on first shots each player takes one of remaining balls and spots it in front of cup and both shoot at same time, just as they did with marked balls. From there on they take turns beginning with the player who pockets ball or is nearest to his cup. A player receives another shot upon sinking his own color ball in his own color cup.

In the event that a player causes a ball to leave the table, his opponent may place this ball anywhere he wishes, and in addition can remove two of his own balls and drop them into his cup as an additional bonus. If a player sinks one of his opponent's balls there is no penalty, but if he sinks one of his own balls into his opponent's cup, or shoots one of his opponent's balls, his opponent may then drop two of his own balls into his own cup. No player is allowed to jump his ball over balls or bumpers in making shots. Penalty for this will be two "free" balls for his opponent. The first player or team to sink all five of their balls is the winner, excepting that player forfeits game if he shoots his last ball into his opponent's cup.

Referee Instructions

1. The referee will, at all times, be completely in charge of the game.
2. The referee makes all decisions which are final unless a protest is supported and proven just, in which case the referee may reverse the decision.
3. The referee will not give advice, or express his opinion on points affecting play.
4. The referee may disqualify a player, at his discretion, for actions not in the best interest of the game.
5. The referee will watch for errors, fouls and interference. He will also direct the scorekeeper and assume responsibility for his accuracy.
6. The referee will not be allowed to wager on the result of a game or tournament.
7. Privilege of selecting the referee is that of the tournament sponsor.

Glossary

Angled: A player is "angled" when the location of the cue ball on the lip of a pocket prevents a clear shot at his object ball because of the interfering end of the cushion.

Bank Shot: A bank shot is when a player drives the cue ball or object ball to the cushion in the course of making the shot.

Break (break shot): Refers to first shot of a game.

Bridge: Refers to the hand that holds and guides the cue shaft, also the type of hold.

Bridge Stick: A cue like stick with a specially shaped plate mounted on the end. This serves as a support for the cue for long or other difficult shots.

Burst: See rules for "41."

Call Shot: Where the player must declare before shooting which ball he intends to pocket and in which pocket ball is to be scored. Some games require that called ball may be scored in any pocket.

Carom: Term describes the glancing of one ball off another or off of a cushion.

Center Ball Hit: Describing a stroke by the cue into the center of the cue ball. This hit causes no English, draw or follow.

Center Spot: The point in the exact center of the table, sometimes marked with spot.

Count: A score.

Cushion (Rail): The resilient (usually gum rubber) cloth covered ridge bordering the playing surface on pool table.

"D": A defined area on snooker tables (see snooker rules).

Dead Ball: A ball that stops "dead" on contact with a cushion or other ball.

Draw: Method of stroking that causes the cue ball to rebound backwards after contact with object ball.

English: Method of stroking that causes cue ball to react to the right or left after contact with an object ball or cushion.

Follow: Method of stroking that causes cue ball to "follow" in the same direction as object ball when struck.

Follow Through: An important motion of the cue on the stroke carrying through the area previously occupied by the cue ball.

Foot Spot: A spot placed in the exact center of a line drawn between the second diamonds from the foot rail.

Foot of Table: The end not marked with the makers name plate or on tables with ball returns, the end that the balls return to.

Frozen: This term is used when 2 balls are touching or "frozen." Term also applies when ball is touching a cushion.

Full Ball Hit: Describe direct full face contact of object ball by cue ball as opposed to "thin" hit.

Head of Table: Opposite of foot (see foot of table).

Head Spot: Corresponding point of foot spot near head of table (see foot spot).

Head String: An imaginary direct line across the table that bisects the head spot.

High Run: Pertains to the highest number of balls scored in one inning.

In Hand: Cue ball "in hand" pertains to the times when player may shoot from anywhere behind the head string as at the beginning of a game or after a cue ball scratch.

Inning: The time between the beginning of a player's turn and the time his turn is ended by missing, fouling, winning, etc.

Kiss: A carom.

Lag or Lagging: Method of determining order of play. Players shoot a ball from behind the head string to the foot rail. Player's ball coming to rest nearest the head rail is winner and has choice of breaking or assigning break to his opponent.

Live Ball: Refers to a ball still spinning or in motion, also a ball legally in play.

Long String: An imaginary line from the foot spot to the center of the foot rail (see rules for rotation).

Miscue: A stroke where the cue tip does not hit the cue ball squarely enough and glances off without driving the cue ball on its desired course. Often caused by not enough chalk on tip, improperly shaped tip or attempt at too much English.

Push Shot: A pushing or shoving action of the cue ball when shooting. This shot is legal in pool but cue must not contact ball twice. Shot must be one continuous motion. Legality of a push shot is up to the referee.

Rack: A triangular form of wood or plastic used to group the balls on the foot spot for the beginning of games. "Rack" also refers to the group of balls themselves when set up on the table.

Rail: The part of the pool table surrounding the playing surface to which the cushions are attached.

Run: Consecutive scores in an inning.

Safety: A defensive action taken when player has no prospective shot on the table. He shoots the cue ball to a spot where hopefully his opponent will also be stymied. When making a safety the player must drive an object ball to a cushion, drive the cue ball to a cushion after striking an object ball or pocket an object ball. Failure is a foul.

Scratch: Pocketing of the cue ball. Check scratch rulings for particular games.

Spot Shot: A shot in which the player is shooting at a ball that has been spotted.

Spotting: The placing of balls as required according to the rules of the particular game.

Stop Shot: A stroke that causes the cue ball to stop dead upon contacting the object ball.

Cues and Their Care

The cue stick is what carries a players wishes to the game. Therefore its importance cannot be over-stressed. I advise players to find a cue you like, take care of it and it will take care of you.

Weight of a 57″ regulation cue can vary from 11-22 oz. but most are 17-21 oz. There is no flat rule on what weight is best for a person. This question has to be answered individually through trial and error.

Most well made cues have shafts of hard straight grain maple chosen for its stable and warp resistance characteristics. The butt sections are usually of a heavier wood. Woods commonly used are rosewood, ebony, walnut and birdseye maple.

The 4 prongs or "points" on many cues are not merely decorative. They provide a greater holding surface for the glue, and make the cue stronger structurally. They also serve to absorb and dissipate the shock generated when the tiny cue tip strikes the ball. Without the prongs a cue might feel somewhat like a baseball bat when held the wrong way.

Many cues also have vari-colored wood inlays at the prongs. These are different types of softer

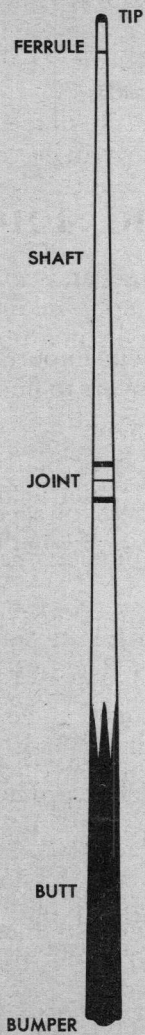

TIP

FERRULE

SHAFT

JOINT

BUTT

BUMPER

Figure 19

woods. Besides being decorative they provide extra shock absorbing qualities to the cue.

The "balance" of a cue is often referred to but seldom understood. A finely balanced cue will have its balance point 16″ to 20″ from the butt end of the cue. More difficult to detect but still important, a well balanced cue will have its weight evenly distributed along its length.

The taper will also be even and sure. A well balanced cue will give you a smoother, easier stroke with greater feel and control. I once heard a new player exclaim upon taking his first shot with a good cue, "This feels like power steering." . . . and it does.

The ferrule (figure 19) on a cue is primarily to absorb shock. Without it the cue end would "spread." Ferrules may be made of ivory, plastic or fiber. Ivory is not particularly any better than plastic or fiber but it provides a classy "look" to the knowing eye. Some breakage is also common with ivory, so for this reason plus its great cost, 99% of all cues today are equipped with plastic or fiber ferrules.

Jointed cues are designated for the player who desires a personal cue that he can take wherever he goes. All top quality cues are jointed but all jointed cues are not top quality. . . . If you know what I mean.

Jointed cues will generally have fancier butt treatments than one piece cues. Wrappings of Nylon, leather, or Irish linen are widely used. Intricate hand carvings and mother-of-pearl inlays are also seen. Besides eye appeal these various treatments give the player a better grip on the cue and help compensate for moisture from the players

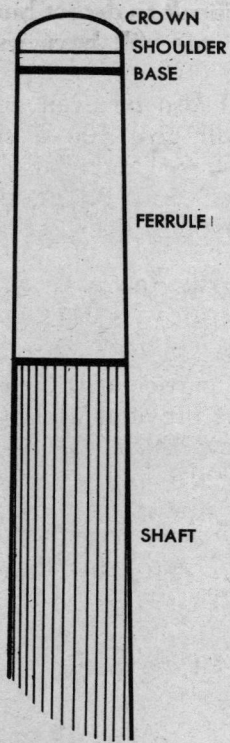

CROWN
SHOULDER
BASE

FERRULE

SHAFT

Figure 20

hand. Irish linen is the most popular wrap among the top pros. It has the unique property of always "feeling" the same whether you are playing in a humid room in the tropics or in a frigid northern city. Irish linen is costly and mostly found only on the very expensive cues.

A player should avoid, when possible, "breaking" with his personal jointed cue. The great shock on the cue can only weaken and loosen the joint, loosen the ferrule and flatten the tip. Greatest accuracy is not required on an "open" break and a house cue will usually do fine.

Jointed cues should be kept in specially made carrying cases. The case will protect the cue from damage and help protect it from warping. Cases are not expensive for what they do and most dealers carry a large selection.

Cue tips are not usually given the attention they deserve. Players who have never maintained their cue tips are always surprised at the effect a good tip has on their game.

Tips come in tan or blue "chrome" leather with both having similar playing qualities. Thickness is one measure of a good tip along with the right texture. A good tip should be:

A. Properly crowned.
B. Resilient yet firm.
C. Slightly "roughed."
D. Well chalked.

The proper "crown" on the tip (Figure 20) is necessary for fullest possible contact on the cue ball. Simple cue tip crowning tools do the best job on this.

Imported tips (usually from France) have many advantages over the common American-made tips. The hides are chosen far more carefully and only the finest parts of those chosen are used. The tips are actually pressed by hand, one at a time. This insures that each tip will have uniform texture and will not spread or flatten. A fiber backing is laminated to the tip as another spreading preventive. Tips made in this fashion will hold their shape, last much longer and play better than machine made, massed produced tips.

Cue Tip Replacement:

1. Prepare cue end by sanding off old glue and leather remnants. Cut tip sander is best for this but sanding block, used carefully will do. Note: It is important that prepared cue end be absolutely flat.
2. Prepare cue tip by roughing up the smooth back on sandpaper. Make 3 or 4 "crosscuts" on the tip back with a sharp knife.
3. Apply cement and let dry a few minutes until glue is tacky.
4. Position tip on cue and press lightly until glue "beads" at edges. Secure lightly with cue tip clamp. Note: Do not force all glue out by pressing too hard on tip.
5. When glue is dry, trim excess glue and leather by stroking shaft and tip with fine sandpaper. Finish with fine steel wool. Note: It is important that sides of finished tip be absolutely flush with sides of cue.
6. If the tip is much bigger than cue end, trim by inverting cue on working surface, holding firmly

and cutting excess off with sharp knife. Be careful to hold knife blade flat against shaft so that cuts will follow the "line" of the cue shaft. After trimming with knife finish as in step #5.

7. Shape tip into proper crown with crowning tool or sandpaper. Be careful when shaping the crown on your tip, to leave a sharp definite "shoulder" at least ⅛" above the ferrule. (Figure 20.)

Equipment Specifications

POOL TABLE SPECIFICATIONS:

Sizes:

Pool Tables	4x8 and 4½x9
Snooker Tables	4½x9 and 5x10

Playing Surface:

4x8	44x88 to 46x92
4½x9	50x100
5x10	56x112

Height:

31″ to 32″ from floor to top of rail

Pool Table Pocket Openings:

Measured between "points" of cushions.

Corner pocket	4⅞″ to 5⅛″
Side pocket	5⅜″ to 5⅝″

Snooker Table Pocket Openings:

Measured between widest part of slate openings.

Corner pocket	3⅜″ to 3⅝″
Side pocket	4⅛″ to 4⁵⁄₁₆″

BALL SPECIFICATIONS:

Pool Balls: 6 oz. 2¼" Diameter

Snooker Balls: 6 oz. 2⅛" diameter

CUE SPECIFICATIONS:

Length: Pool cues 57", Snooker cues 60"

Weight: Pool and Snooker cues 14-22 oz.

Tip Diameter: Pool and Snooker cues 11 to 15mm

Cloth Replacement

BED CLOTH

Lay the bed cloth over the top of the bed, with the playing surface up.

Leave enough cloth at head and at the left side for tacking, into bed. Leave the balance of the cloth over-hang at the right side and the foot.

NOTE: Tacking can be done with ordinary tacks or with a hand stapler.

Tack cloth to bed at (1) with two tacks about two inches apart.

Next: Stretch cloth across the table and tack at (2), with two tacks, two inches apart.

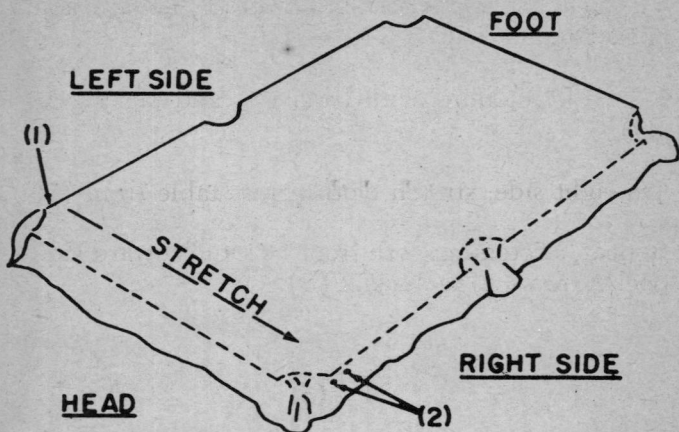

LEFT SIDE

FOOT

(1)

STRETCH

HEAD

RIGHT SIDE

(2)

Stretch cloth from (1) to (3), and tack bed, at left side of table.

Next: Stretch cloth across from (3) and pull from (2) tacking cloth at (4).

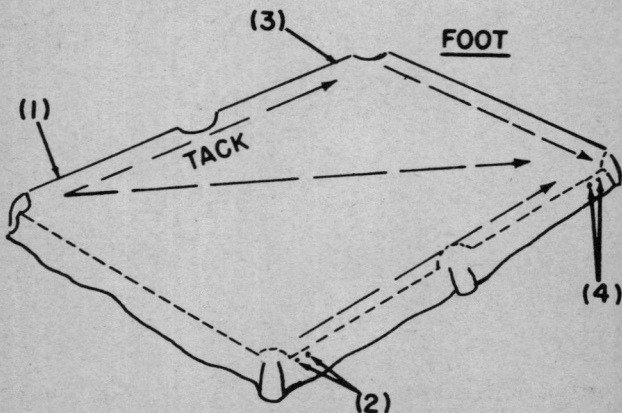

(3)

FOOT

(1)

TACK

(4)

(2)

84

On the left side, stretch cloth from (1) toward side pocket and tack at (5).

Repeat, stretching cloth from (3) and tacking at (6).

On right side, stretch cloth across table from (5) and toward side pocket from (2) and tack at (7). Repeat, stretching cloth from (6) and toward side pocket from (4) tacking at (8).

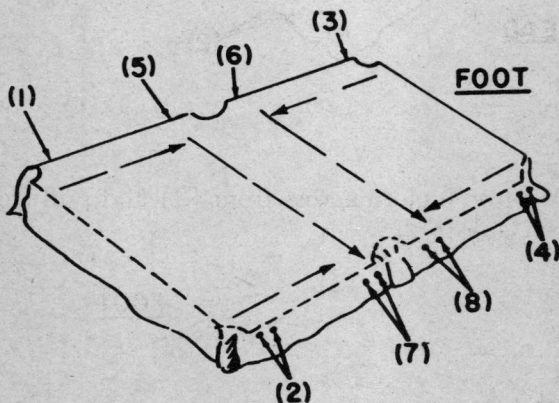

Cut a short slit in cloth, in the center of the side pocket opening (9) and pull cloth downward, with grasp above slit, and tack below pocket opening.

Stretch cloth across table from (9). Repeat pocket operation at (10).

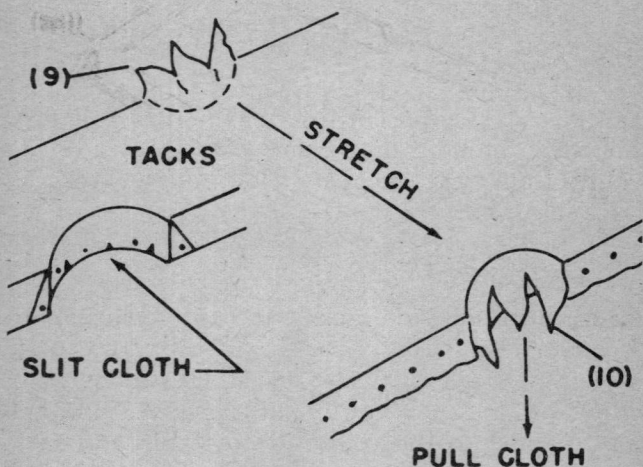

TACKS

STRETCH

(9)

SLIT CLOTH

PULL CLOTH

(10)

At head of table, tack cloth at (11). Maintain a uniform overhang of cloth.

Stretch cloth from (11) toward (12) and tack along bed maintaining an even amount of cloth at head end.

Stretch cloth from (11) to foot end and tack at (13).

Stretch cloth from (12) and (13) toward (14) and tack along bed.

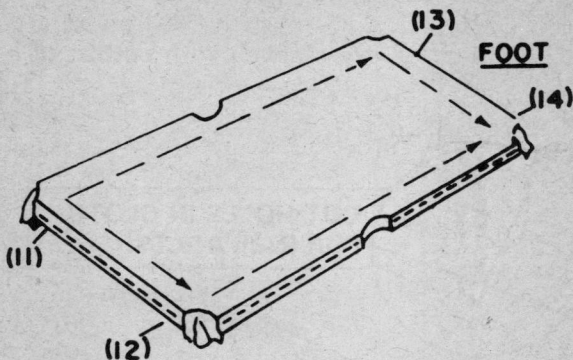

Tack entire left side, tacks two (15) inches apart.
Keep an even margin of cloth. (16) Next complete
tacking of head end. (17). Now stretch cloth
toward foot end of table, and tack. (18) Stretch
cloth across to the right side of table and tack.

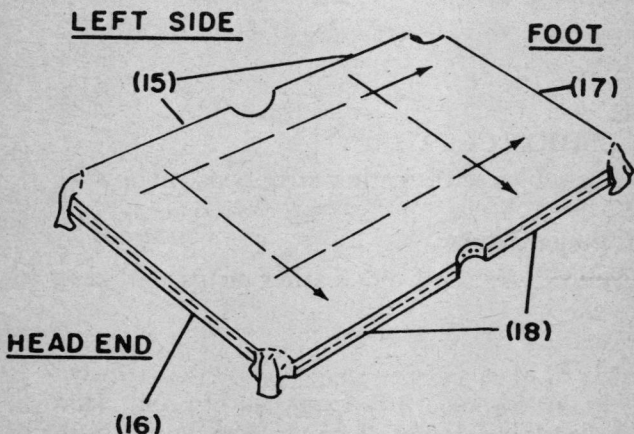

cloth is approximately ¾" from the end of the feather strip. Tap feather strip in place.

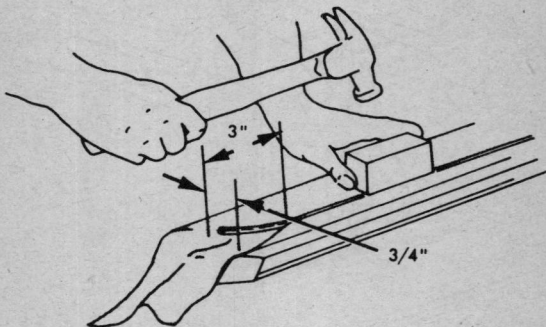

C. For side pockets, start approximately 3" from end of rail and pull cloth toward rubber cushion until the edge of the cloth is approximately ½" from the end of the feather strip. Tap feather strip in place.

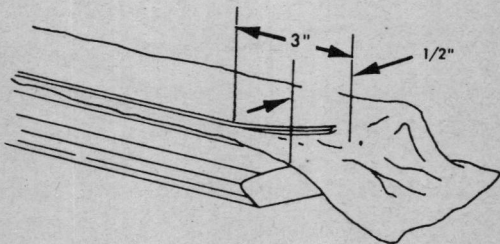

D. Pull cloth tight and tap feather strip in place, then trim cloth along cushion side of feather strip. Fold cloth over cushion and tap full length of feather strip flush with rail cap.

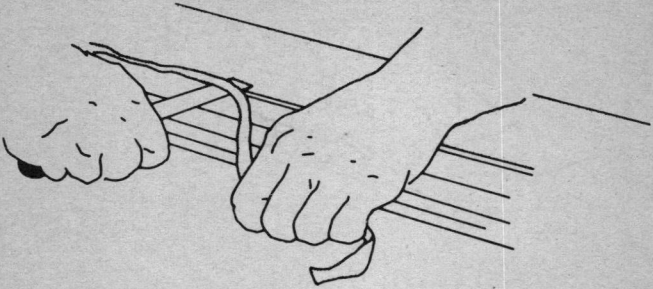

3. Tack Cloth

A. Pull cloth tightly downward and tack with four tacks along bottom rail. Pull cloth tightly over end of rail and tack with three tacks in groove back of cushion reinforcing pad.

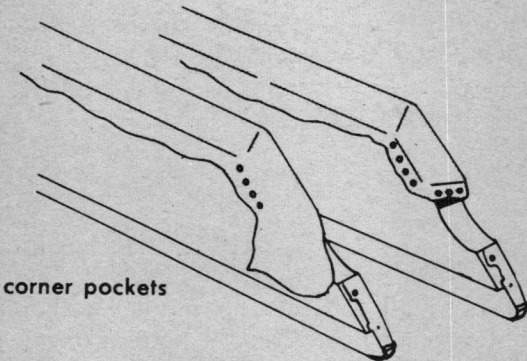

corner pockets

B. For side pockets, stretch cloth firmly over nose of cushion toward the bottom without distorting cushion shape. Tack cloth to rail bottom for approximately 2" from pocket opening.

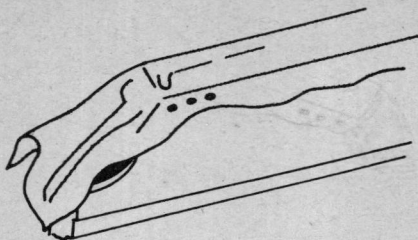

C. Snip cloth at nose and pull small strip down to groove, tack in place as shown. Then snip excess cloth leaving enough for small fold at the top as shown.

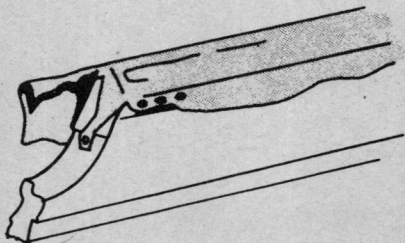

D. Hold small fold at top in place, then fold entire piece over. Tack at bottom of rail with (3) tacks and (3) at groove. Stretch balance of cloth tightly over cushion and tack at bottom of rail, starting at the center, and working toward the ends. Space tacks about 2″ apart. Be sure cloth is snug, but not tight enough to alter shape of the cushion.

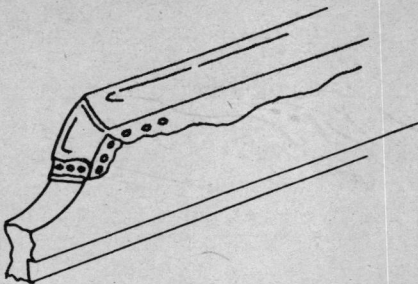

E. Trim excess cloth from rail.

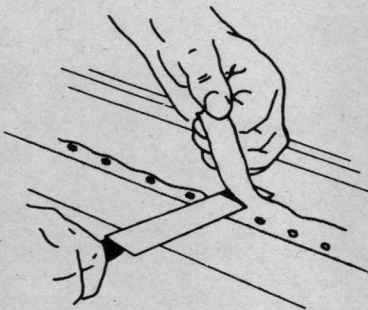

CUSHION CLOTH
(For tables with removable cushions)

1. First remove the old cloth and all of old staples.
    Be careful to note how the cloth has been
    applied. It will be helpful to you in replace-
    ment of the new covering. Cut the cloth ap-

proximately 6 inches longer than the rail and allow the ends to extend about 3 inches over each end of the rail as in Figure "A." Staple the cloth to the top edge of the back of the rail starting and stopping the staples about 3 inches from the ends. The cloth should be allowed to lap over the back about ½ inch and stretched in the length while driving staples about ¾ of an inch apart.

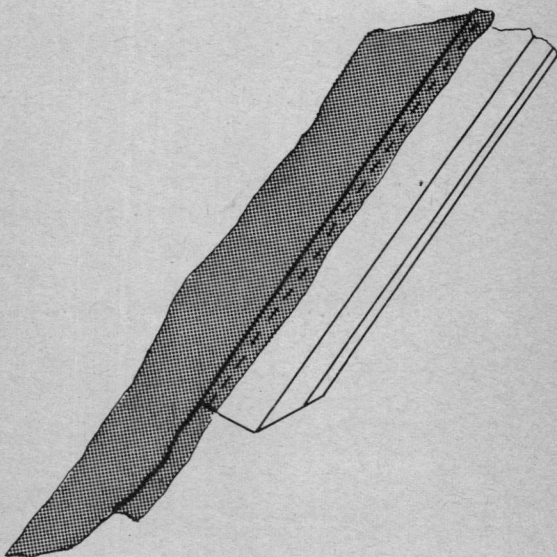

2. Second—pull the cloth tightly around the front of the rail and staple to the bottom edge of the back of the rail in the same manner as Step 1. If the cloth is too wide, the extra material can

be trimmed off after the second stapling operation. This trim should be about ¼ of an inch from the staples as shown in Figure "B."

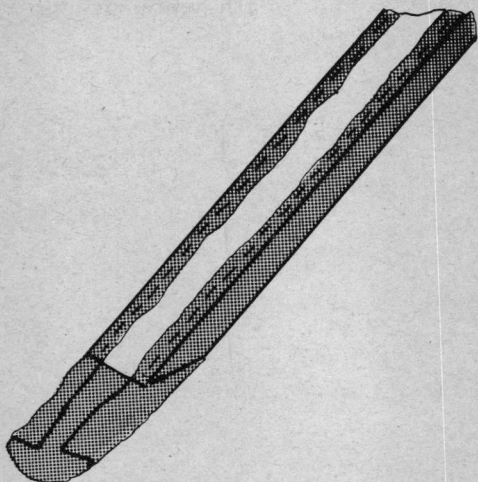

FIGURE B

3. For corner pockets, stretch the cloth over the angled face of the rail and staple to the back allowing small even wrinkles as shown in Figure "C" on the back side. NOTE—care should be taken to stretch before wrapping around to the back side so that the sharp part of the angle cut will not tear or cut the cloth.

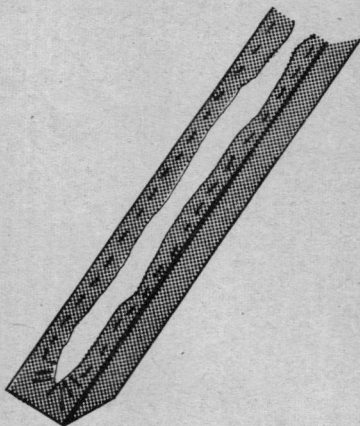

4. For side pockets—finish stapling the back edge and slit as shown in Figure "D." Pull the front section over the nose of the rail tightly and staple to the back side. Snip the excess material off leaving enough for a small fold which should be pulled down across the front and stapled to the bottom of the rail as shown in Figure "E."

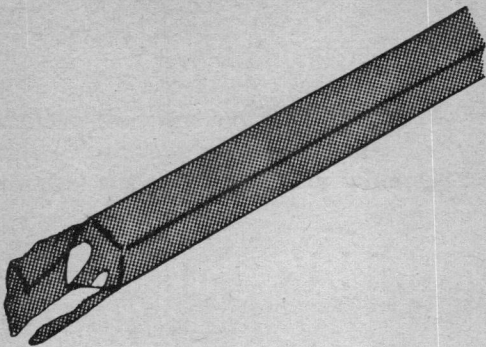

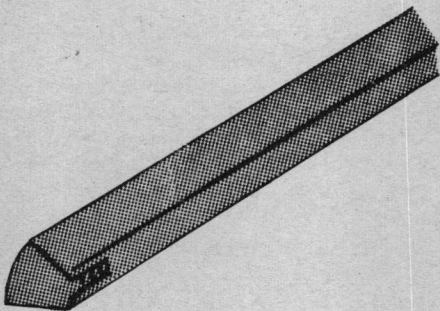

Be sure all excess cloth is snipped off to allow the cushion rail to set tightly when fastened on to top rail and bed.

World's Billiards Champions and Records

WORLD 18.2 BALKLINE CHAMPIONS

Maurice Vignaux . . 1903-05	Willie Hoppe 1910-20
Geo. F. Slosson 1906	Jake Schaefer 1921-22
Geo. B. Sutton 1906-07	Willie Hoppe 1923-24
Willie Hoppe 1907	Edward Horemans* . . 1925
Jacob Schaefer, Sr. . . . 1907	Jake Schaefer 1925
Geo. F. Slosson 1908	Erich Hagenlocher . . . 1926
Geo. B. Sutton 1908	Welker Cochran 1927
Ora C. Morningstar. . . 1909	Edward Horemans . . . 1928
Calvin Demarest 1909	Jake Schaefer 1929-33
Harry P. Cline 1910	Welker Cochran 1934

*Disputed match—Schaefer won play-off.

WORLD 18.1 BALKLINE CHAMPIONS

Maurice Vignaux . . 1903-05	Willie Hoppe 1909-11
Willie Hoppe 1906	George B. Sutton 1912
George B. Sutton 1907	Ora C. Morningstar. . . 1913
Willie Hoppe 1907	Willie Hoppe 1914-26
Jacob Schaefer, Sr. . . . 1908	Jake Schaefer, Jr. . 1926-27
Geo. B. Sutton* 1908	Willie Hoppe 1927
Geo. F. Slosson 1908	

*By forfeit.

WORLD 14.1 BALKLINE CHAMPIONS

1914 .... Willie Hoppe

WORLD 28.2 BALKLINE CHAMPION

1937 .... Jake Schaefer, Jr.

WORLD 71.2 BALKLINE CHAMPION

1938 .... Willie Hoppe

WORLD THREE-CUSHION CHAMPION

Leon Magnus 1878	Alfredo DeOro 1919
W. H. Catton 1899	R. L. Cannafax 1919
Eugene Carter 1900	John Layton 1920
Lloyd Jevne 1900	Augie Kieckhefer 1921
Harry P. Cline 1907	John Layton 1921-23
John Daly 1908	Tiff Denton 1923
Thos. Hueston 1908	R. L. Cannafax 1924
Alfredo DeOro.... 1908-09	R. L. Cannafax 1925
Fred Eames 1910	Otto Reiselt 1926-27
Alfredo DeOro 1910	Augie Kieckhefer 1927
John Daly 1910	Otto Reiselt 1928
Thos. Hueston 1910	John Layton 1928-29
John Daly 1911	John Layton 1930
Alfredo DeOro 1911	Arthur Thurnblad ... 1931
Joe Carney 1912	Augie Kieckhefer 1932
John Horgan 1912	Welker Cochran 1933
Alfredo DeOro ... 1913-14	John Layton 1934
George Moore 1915	Welker Cochran 1935
Wm. H. Huey 1915	Willie Hoppe 1936
Alfredo DeOro 1916	Welker Cochran 1937
Chas. Ellis 1916	Welker Cochran 1938
Chas. McCourt 1916	Joe Chamaco 1939
Hugh Heal 1916	Welker Cochran 1944
Geo. Moore 1916	Welker Cochran 1945
Chas. McCourt 1917	Willie Hoppe 1947-52
R. L. Cannafax 1917	Ray Kilgore 1953
Alfredo DeOro ... 1917-18	No Tournament sanctioned
Augie Kieckhefer.. 1918-19	after above date.

Three Cushion Billiard Records

HIGH RUNS

1915 . . Chas. Morin . . Tournament (Pro) 18
1919 . . Tiff Denton . . Tournament (World's) 17
1926 . . John Layton . . Inter-state League 18
1927 . . Willie Hoppe. . American League 20
1928 . . Willie Hoppe. . Exhibition vs. C. C. Peterson 25
1930 . . Gus Copulos . . Tournament (World's) 17
1936 . . Willie Hoppe. . Match play 15
1939 . . Joe Chamaco. . National League* 18
1940 . . Tiff Denton . . . Tournament† (World's) . . .17
1945 . . Willie Hoppe. . Match play†† 20

*No safeties allowed. †Safeties allowed. ††No safeties; optional cue ball first shot of inning.

HIGH AVERAGES (BEST GAME)

1925 . . Otto Reiselt . . . . . 50 in 16 Innings—Interstate
                                              League
1925 . . Otto Reiselt . . . . . 100 in 57 Innings—Interstate
                                              League
1925 . . Otto Reiselt . . . . . 150 in 104 Innings—Interstate
                                              League
1930 . . John Layton . . . . . 50 in 23 Innings—Tournamer

1939 . . Joe Chamaco . . . . 50 in 23 Innings—National
                                              League*
1940 . . Jay N. Bozeman. . 50 in 23 Innings—Tournamer

1947 . . Willie Hoppe . . . . 50 in 21 Innings—Match
  *No safeties.   †Safeties.

HIGH GRAND AVERAGE

1950 . . Willie Hoppe . . . . Tournament. 1.33

WORLD POCKET BILLIARD CHAMPIONS

Cyrille Dion......1878-80	Jerome Keogh 1910
Gottlieb Whalstrom...1881	Alfredo DeOro....1910-12
Albert Frey 1882-83	R. J. Ralph 1912
J. L. Malone 1884	Alfredo DeOro 1913
Albert Frey 1886-87	Bennie Allen 1913-15
J. L. Malone (forfeit) .1887	Emmet Blankenship ..1916
Alfredo DeOro ...1887-88	John Layton 1916
Frank Powers 1888	Frank Taberski....1916-18
Albert Frey 1889	Ralph Greenleaf ..1919-24
Alfredo DeOro 1889	Frank Taberski 1925
H. Manning 1890	Ralph Greenleaf 1926
Frank Powers (forfeit) 1891	Erwin Rudolph 1926
Alfredo DeOro ...1892-94	Thos. Hueston 1926
Wm. Clearwater 1895	Frank Taberski 1927
Alfredo DeOro 1895	Ralph Greenleaf ..1927-28
Frank Stewart (forfeit) 1896	Frank Taberski......1928
Grant Eby 1897	Ralph Greenleaf 1929
Jerome Keogh 1897	Frank Taberski 1929
Wm. Clearwater 1898	Erwin Rudolph 1930
Jerome Keogh 1898	Ralph Greenleaf ..1930-32
Alfredo DeOro..1899-1900	Erwin Rudolph ...1933-34
Frank Sherman 1901	Andrew Ponzi 1935
Alfredo DeOro 1901	James Caras 1936
Wm. Clearwater 1902	Ralph Greenleaf 1937
Grant Eby 1902	James Caras 1938
Alfredo DeOro 1903	James Caras 1939
Alfredo DeOro 1904	Andrew Ponzi 1940
Jerome Keogh (forfeit) 1905	Willie Mosconi 1941
Alfredo DeOro 1905	Erwin Rudolph 1941
Thos. Hueston (forfeit) 1905	Irving Crane 1942
Thos. Hueston 1906	Willie Mosconi 1942
John Horgan 1906	Andrew Ponzi 1943
Jerome Keogh 1906	Willie Mosconi ...1943-45
Thos. Hueston 1907	Irving Crane 1946
Thos. Hueston 1908	Willie Mosconi ...1946-48
Frank Sherman 1908	James Caras 1949
Alfredo DeOro 1908	Willie Mosconi ...1950-53
Chas. Weston 1909	No Tournament 1954
John Kling 1909	Irving Crane 1955
Thos. Hueston 1910	Willie Mosconi ...1955-57

UNITED STATES OPEN

Irving Crane 1966 Chicago, Illinois—Runner-up—Joe Balsis
Jimmy Caras 1967 St. Louis, Missouri—Runner-up—Luther
Lassiter

RECORDS—14.1 POCKET BILLIARDS

1929 . . Ralph Greenleaf — Tournament — Detroit . . High
run 126
1934 . . Andrew Ponzi—Match—New York. . High run 153
1935 . . Bennie Allen—Tournament—New York. . High run
125
1935 . . Geo Kelly—Tournament—Minneapolis. . High run
125
1929 . . Ralph Greenleaf—Tournament—Detroit
High Single average 63
1929 . . Ralph Greenleaf—Tournament—Detroit
(5 x 10 table) High Individual grand average
11.02
Best Game—(World's Championship) Ralph Greenleaf, 2
Innings, against Frank Taberski, Detroit, Dec.
1929.
1939 . . Andrew Ponzi (League play) . . . . High run 127
1939 . . Irving Crane—Run of 309 Exhibition—Layton,
Utah
Best Game—Willie Mosconi, 2 innings against Arthur Cranfield (5 x 10 table) 1941.
1945 . . Willie Mosconi (Match-Single Game) . . High run
127
1946 . . James Caras (Match-Single Game) . . High run 127
1950 . . Willie Mosconi—Tournament—Chicago
(4½ x 9 table) High grand average 18.34
Best Game—Willie Mosconi, 2 innings against George
Chenier at Boston, Mass., 1952.
Best Game—(World's Championship) Willie Mosconi, 2
innings against Luther Lassiter, San Francisco,
Mar., 1953.
1951 . . Irving Crane—Run of 160 vs. Willie Mosconi
(4½ x 9) Kansas City, Missouri.
1954 . . Willie Mosconi (Exh. High Run) Springfield,
Ill. 526

1954 . . Joe Procita—(5 x 10 table)—Philadelphia. . . . . . .
        High run 182
1956 . . Willie Mosconi, 1 inning (def)
        Jimmy Moore—Kinston, N.C. . . . . . . .Run 150
1965 . . Joe Balsis—Burbank, Calif. run 150 vs. Harold
        Worst—1 inning.
1966 . . Irving Crane—Run of 150 U. S. Open Finals vs.
        Balsis, Chicago, Illinois.

RED BALL CHAMPION

1907-44........Chas C. Peterson

HIGH RUN:

1915 ....Chas. C. Peterson.................54

HIGH AVERAGE:

1915 ....Chas C. Peterson 5.33

AMATEUR CHAMPIONS & RECORDS
18.2 BALKLINE

H. A. Wright........	1909	Percy Collins†	1923
E. W. Gardner	1910	E. T. Appleby	1924
J. F. Poggenburg	1911	F. S. Appleby......	1925
M. D. Brown	1912	John Clinton 1926-28	
Jos. Mayer	1913	E. T. Appleby‡	1929
E. W. Gardner	1914	Percy Collins‡	1929
Nathan Hall	1915	M. C. Walgren‡	1929
C. Huston	1916	Percy Collins	1930
Dave McAndless	1917	E. T. Appleby	1931
Percy Collins	1918	Albert Poensgren§ ...1932	
C. Heddon	1919	Albert Poensgren	1933
E. T. Appleby	1920	Edmund Soussa ..1934-36	
Percy Collins	1921	Edmund Soussa ..1937-40	
E. T. Appleby*	1922		

*International champion.   †Nat. 18.1 champion—F. S. Appleby.
‡Amateur Billiard Assn.   §(Germany) World's Champion.

THREE CUSHION CHAMPIONS

Pierre Maupome	 1910	Chas. Jordan	 1929
Charles Morin	 1911	Max Shimon	 1929
Arthur Newman	 1919	Joseph Hall	 1930
W. B. Huey	 1920	Max Shimon	 1930
Earl Lookabaugh	 1921	R. B. Harper	 1930
Frank Flemming	 1922	Frank Flemming	 1931
Robert M. Lord	 1923	Edward Lee	 1931-35
Frank Flemming	 1924	Edward Lee*	 1936
Dr. A. J. Harris	. . 1925-26	A. Primeau	 1937
Robert M. Lord	 1927	Gene Deardorff	 1938
Dr. L. P. Macklin	. . . 1927	Gene Deardorff	. . 1939-40
J. N. Bozeman	 1928	Edward Lee	 1946

*World's Champion.

POCKET BILLIARD CHAMPIONS

A. Hyman	 1912	J. H. Shoemaker	 1930
J. H. Shoemaker	 1913	Robt. Cole	 1931
No Tournament	 1914	J. H. Shoemaker*	. . . 1931
J. H. Shoemaker	. . 1915-22	E. Fagin	 1932
E. F. Reynolds	 1923	J. H. Shoemaker*	. . . 1932
J. H. Shoemaker	 1924	E. Fagin	 1933
Carl A. Vaughan	 1925	J. H. Shoemaker*	 1933
Clarence Hurd	 1926	J. H. Shoemaker	. . 1934-35
J. H. Shoemaker	 1927	E. C. Rogers	 1936-37
J. Collins	 1928	Arthur Cranfield	. . 1938-40
Cy. Yellin	 1929		

*By challenge.

WOMEN CHAMPIONS

PROFESSIONAL
14.1 POCKET BILLIARDS

Ruth McGinnis.... 1932-50
Dorothy Wise .... 1967 St. Louis, Missouri—High Run 40

INTERCOLLEGIATE BILLIARDS
The first Intercollegiate Billiard Match
"Grand Trial of Skill"
July 25, 1860, Worcester, Mass.
Between

Freshman class of Harvard University
Freshman class of Yale University

Forthingham and Stackpole ....Harvard
Sheffield and Beam ....Yale

	Score	High Run	Aver.
Harvard	800	45	6.61
Yale	720	41	5.12

ENGLAND

1865-66 Team Championship:

Cambridge	500	Oxford	496
Oxford	330	Cambridge	500

Single Championship:

Oxford	500	Cambridge	461

MODERN PLAY

1931 . . University of Wisconsin straight rail Billiard
Championship for the Chas. C. Peterson trophy
H. Platz, Winner

Intercollegiate team and individual championships at straight rail, three cushion and pocket billiards, sanctioned by The Billiard Congress of America, and sponsored by the National Billiard Council.

INTERCOLLEGIATE KEY SHOT TEAM CHAMPIONS

FIVE MAN TEAMS—STRAIGHT RAIL:

University of Michigan 1932	St. Joseph's College . 1947
University of Michigan 1933	Ohio State 1948
Michigan State College 1934	Ohio State 1949
University of Wisconsin 1935	No Tournament . . 1950
Purdue University . . 1936	University of Utah . . 1951
Cornell University . . 1937	Michigan State Normal Col.
Cornell University . . 1938	 1952
University of Wisconsin 1939	University of Michigan 1953°
University of Michigan 1940	University of Cincinnati
Cornell University . . 1941	University of Utah . 1954°
University of Wisconsin 1942	Michigan State Coleege 1955°
University of Florida . 1943	Michigan State College 1956°
Cornell University . . 1944	Suolk University . . 1957°
No Tournament . 1945-46	Team Play discontinued after 1957

FIVE MAN TEAMS—THREE CUSHIONS:

Michigan State College 1935	Indiana University . 1948
Cornell University . . 1936	Cornell University . . 1949
Iowa State College . 1937	Ohio State 1950
University of Wisconsin 1938	University of Michigan 1951
University of Utah . 1939	Michigan State College 1952
University of Michigan 1940	Ohio State University 1953°
University of Buffalo . 1942	University of Florida 1954*
University of Florida . 1943	University of Oregon 1955°
University of Florida . 1944	Michigan State College 1956°
No Tournament . 1945-46	University of Florida 1957°
University of Florida . 1947	Team Play discontinued after 1957°

FIVE MAN TEAMS—POCKET BILLIARDS:

University of Michigan	1936	University of Michigan	1947
University of Wisconsin	1937	University of Florida .	1948
University of Florida .	1938	Eastern Kentucky . .	1949
University of Buffalo .	1939	Ohio State	1950
University of Michigan	1940	University of Notre Dame	1951
University of Florida .	1941	University of Wyoming	1952
University of Florida .	1942	University of Wyoming	1953*
University of Minnesota	1943	University of Arizona	1955*
University of Indiana .	1944	Michigan State College	1956*
No Tournament .	1945-46	Team Play discontinued after 1957	

*Three man teams

CO-ED TEAM CHAMPIONS (POCKETS)

1942	University of Wyoming
1943	South Dakota State College
1944	Colorado State College of Education
1948	Rhode Island State
1949	Ohio State
1950	(No tournament)
1951	South Dakota State College
1952	University of Minnesota
1953	Purdue University
1954	Oregon State College
1955	University of Arizona
1956	University of Arizona
1957	State University of Iowa
1958	State University of Iowa
1959	Purdue University

Team Play discontinued after 1959

INTERCOLLEGIATE INDIVIDUAL CHAMPIONS

STRAIGHT RAIL BILLIARDS:

1937.... Leroy Lillisand........ University of Wisconsin
1938.... John O. Miller .... University of Wisconsin
1939.... Carleton H. Sheeley .... Cornell University
1940.... John O. Miller .... University of Wisconsin
1941.... Ted Davis .... University of Florida
1942.... David Vig .... University of Wisconsin
1943.... R. McCloskey .... University of Michigan
1944.... G. Neuberg .... Cornell University
1945-46. (No tournament)
1947.... Thos. Hines .... University of Wisconsin
1948.... Gordon Howe .... University of Wisconsin
1949.... Thos. Hines .... University of Wisconsin
1950.... (No tournament)
1951.... Conrado Roa .... University of Michigan
1952.... Dan Fader .... Cornell University
1953.... Merle R. Osborn...... Michigan State College
1954.... Bill Robinson .... University of Florida
1955.... Robert Blackham........... University of Utah
1956.... Tulio Carta.......... Michigan State College
1957.... Billy Snowden .... University of Texas
1958.... Jim Perez........... State University of Iowa
1959.... Jim Perez........... State University of Iowa
1960.... Jorge Izaguirre........ Kansas State University
1961.... John Rutan.............. Indiana University
Tournaments discontinued after 1961

THREE CUSHION BILLIARDS:

1938.... Geo. Hansen........... University of Michigan
1939.... Edw. Bergen.............. Iowa State College
1940.... John O. Miller........ University of Wisconsin
1941.... (No tournament)
1942.... M. Colomaio........... University of Buffalo
1943.... Ran Metheney.... .... University of Florida
1944.... W. Rion................ University of Florida
1945-46... (No tournament)
1947.... Leff Mabie.............. University of Florida
1948.... Sol. Ashkenaze........ University of Wisconsin
1949.... Victor Brodsky........ University of California
1950.... Walter Johnson.................... Ohio State
1951.... Larry Gray........... University of Michigan
1952.... Paul Ridout.......... University of Wisconsin
1953.... Ted Conant......... University of Minnesota
1954.... Robert Strange......... Michigan State College
1955.... Robert Strange........ Michigan State College
1956.... Robert Strange....... Michigan State College
1957.... Frank Tajima....... University of Washington
1958.... Harold Murphy........... Iowa State College
1959.... Virgil Pope.......... University of Wisconsin
1960.... Fred Beck................ Purdue University
1961.... William Ervin............ Indiana University
1962.... Douglas Saunders...... University of California
1963.... A. J. Bettles.......... University of California
1964.... A. J. Bettles.......... University of California
1965.... Larry Lawrence...... Western State University
1966.... Bill Kiesler......... Michigan State University
1967.... William "Wiley" Williams.. Louisiana State University

POCKET BILLIARDS:

1937 . . . . John O. Miller . . . . University of Wisconsin
1938 . . . . J. L. Geiger . . . . University of Florida
1939 . . . . Peter Choulas . . . . Colgate University
1940 . . . . John O. Miller . . . . University of Wisconsin
1941 . . . . Lloyd Green . . . . University of Kansas
1942 . . . . Leo Bonimi . . . . Cornell University
1943 . . . . L. Mabie . . . . University of Florida
1944 . . . . J. Zvanya . . . . University of Indiana
1945-46 . (No tournament)
1947 . . . . Leff Mabie . . . . University of Florida
1948 . . . . Jack Brown . . . . University of Utah
1949 . . . . Leroy Kinman . . . . Eastern Kentucky State
1950 . . . . Leroy Kinman . . . . Eastern Kentucky State
1951 . . . . Leroy Kinman . . . . Eastern Kentucky State
1952 . . . . Bill Simms . . . . University of Georgia
1953 . . . . John Beaudette . . . . Michigan State College
1954 . . . . John Beaudette . . . . Michigan State College
1955 . . . . Rodney Boyd . . . . Ohio State University
1956 . . . . Joseph Sapanaro . . . . Suffolk University
1957 . . . . Joseph Sapanaro . . . . Suffolk University
1958 . . . . Lloyd Courter . . . . State Univeristy of Iowa
1959 . . . . Donald Dull . . . . . . State College of Washington
1960 . . . . Henry Parks . . . . Indiana University
1961 . . . . Jim Finucane . . . . University of Notre Dame
1962 . . . . Robert Burke . . . . University of Oregon
1963 . . . . Larry Galloway . . . . Indiana University
1964 . . . . William Hendricks . . . Southern Illinois University
1965 . . . . William Wells . . . . Tulane University
1966 . . . . William Wells . . . . Tulane University
1967 . . . . Richard Baumgarth . . . . Purdue University

CO-ED CHAMPIONS (POCKETS)

1929.... Margaret Anderson....... University of Illinois
1942.... Emily Ann Julian.... South Dakota State College
1943.... Mary Jean Noonan.. South Dakota State College
1944.... Barbara Jackson... Colorado State College of Ed.
1948.... Jeanne Lynch............. Rhode Island State
1949.... Cora Libbey.......... University of Wisconsin
1950.... (No tournament)
1951.... Ramona Fiedler.... South Dakota State College
1952.... Sondra Bilsky.............. Purdue University
1953.... Joanne Skonning........... Purdue University
1954.... Jackie Slusher.......... Oregon State College
1954.... Lee McGary............. University of Oregon
1955.... Judy Ferles............. University of Arizona
1956.... Judy Ferles............. University of Arizona
1957.... No Co-ed Face to Face......................
1958.... No Co-ed Face to Face......................
1959.... Jan Deeter............... Purdue University
1960.... Darlene McCabe........ University of Oregon
1961.... Ann Sidlauskas........... Indiana University
1962.... San Merrick.... Bowling Green State University
1963.... Barbara Watkins. Bowling Green State University
1964.... Barbara Watkins. Bowling Green State University
1965.... Susan Sloan.............. University of Texas
1966.... Linda Randolph........ Iowa State University
1967.... Shirley Glicen........... University of Miami

BOYS' CLUBS OF AMERICA (Pocket Billiard Champions)
INDIVIDUAL CHAMPIONS (JUNIOR)

1945.... Sam Cavaleiri,
Boys' Club, Big Bro. Organ.... Scranton, Pa.
1946.... Don Gratzer, Bedford Boys' Club.. Bedford, Ind.
1947.... Don Gratzer, Bedford Boys' Club.. Bedford, Ind.
1948.... Anthony Venuto, So. Phila. Boys' Club. Phila., Pa.
1949.... Joe Di Salvo, Boys' Club of N.Y... New York City
1950.... Chas. Santore, Hi. Boys' Club.. Philadelphia, Pa.
1951.... Robert Legg,
Princeton Boys' Club........ Princeton, Ind.
1952.... Robert Legg,
Princeton Boys' Club........ Princeton, Ind.
1953.... Michael Doran,
Flatbush Boys' Club........ Brooklyn, N. Y.
1954.... Marvin Goldstein,
Albany Boys' Club............ Albany, N. Y.
1955.... Michael Doran,
Flatbush Boys' Club........ Brooklyn, N. Y.
1956.... William Saunders,
R. W. Brown Boys' Club.... Philadelphia, Pa.
1957.... Raymond Lopez,
Variety Boys' Club........ Los Angeles, Calif.
1958.... Richard Valdez,
Variety Int'l Boys' Club.... Los Angeles, Calif.
1959.... Gilbert McCullin,
Variety Int'l Boys' Club.... Los Angeles, Calif.
1960.... Robert Hata,
Variety Int'l Boys' Club.... Los Angeles, Calif.
1961.... Wendell Ruppe,
Boys' Club of LaHabra...... LaHabra, Calif.
1962.... Mike Meek,
Boys' Club of Santa Ana... Santa, Ana, Calif.
1963.... Richard Szramowski,
Boys' Club of Pittsburgh..... Pittsburgh, Pa.
1964.... Martin Zuban,
Boys' Club of Pittsburgh..... **Pittsburgh, Pa.**
1965.... Daniel Rosek,
Pittsburgh Boys' Club....... Pittsburgh, Pa.
1966.... Dennis Bolella,
Boys' Club of Queens, Long Island City, N. Y.
1967.... Ted Osborn, Dayton Boys' Club... Dayton, Ohio

INDIVIDUAL CHAMPIONS (INTERMEDIATE)

1945-46. Oscar Williams,
        Harlem Boys' Club.........New York, N. Y.
1947.....Bill Gratzer, Bedford Boys' Club..Bedford, Ind.
1948.....John Romano,
        Flatbush Boys' Club........Brooklyn, N. Y.
1949.....Don Gratzner, Bedford Boys' Club.Bedford, Ind.
1950.....Jerry Tiernan,
        Flatbush Boys' Club........Brooklyn, N. Y.
1951.....Salvatore Attardi,
        Tomp. Sq. Boys' Club.......Brooklyn, N. Y.
1952.....Gerald Piccarelli,
        Worcester Boys' Club......Worcester, Mass.
1953.....Robert Legg,
        Princeton Boys' Club........Princeton, Ind.
1954.....Harry Goldstein,
        Albany Boys' Club...........Albany, N. Y.
1955.....John F. Scully,
        Madison Sq. Boys' Club....New York, N. Y.
1956.....Marvin Goldstein,
        Albany Boys' Club...........Albany, N. Y.
1957.....Donald Barnhart, Boys' Club of
        Hollywood, Inc...........Hollywood, Calif.
1958.....Raymond Lopez,
        Variety Int'l Boys' Club...Los Angeles, Calif.
1959.....Allen Shipes,
        Boys' Clubs of Augusta, Inc....Augusta, Ga.
1960.....Gilbert McCullen,
        Variety Int'l Boys' Club...Los Angeles, Calif.
1961.....Fritz Seibt. Boys' Clubs of Detroit.Detroit, Mich.
1962.....Gilbert A. McCullen,
        Variety Boys' Club........Los Angeles, Calif.
1963.....Gary Peel,
        Boys' Clubs of Augusta, Inc....Augusta, Ga.
1964.....Robert Atchley
        (Queens)..........Long Island City, N. Y.
1965.....Brian Halton, Variety Boys' Club.Houston, Texas
1966.....Donald Beck—Waco Boys' Club...Waco, Texas
1967.....Jim Woods,
        Boys' Club Harbor Area...Costa Mesa, Calif.

INDIVIDUAL CHAMPIONS (SENIOR)

1961.... Edward Kuzmic,
      The Boys' Club of Pittsburgh. Pittsburgh, Penn.
1962.... Henry Miyashiro,
      Variety Boys' Club......Los Angeles, Calif.
1963.... Robert Lewkowicz,
      Boys' Club of Pittsburgh......Pittsburgh, Pa.
1964.... Robert Lewkowicz
      Boys' Club of Pittsburgh......Pittsburgh, Pa.
1965.... Robert Atchley
      Queens Boys' Club....Long Island City, N. Y.
1966.... Ron Bidleman, Boys' Club of Seattle
      & Kings Co............West Seattle, Wash.
1967.... Jimmy Church,
      Boys' Club of Temple.........Temple, Tex.

(Pocket Billiard Team Champions)
(National Key Shot Tournaments)

TEAM CHAMPIONS—JUNIOR DIVISION

1956.... Variety International Boys' Club
      Los Angeles, Calif.
1957.... Variety International Boys' Club
      Los Angeles, Calif.
1958.... Variety International Boys' Club
      Los Angeles, Calif.
1959.... Wissahickon Boys' Club......Philadelphia, Pa.
1960.... Variety International Boys' Club
      Los Angeles, Calif.
1961.... Boys' Club of Utica, Inc..........Utica, N. Y.
1962.... Boys' Club of Santa Ana......Santa Ana, Calif.
1963.... Boys' Club of Pittsburgh........Pittsburgh, Pa.
1964.... Boys' Club of Pittsburgh........Pittsburgh, Pa.
1965.... Boys' Club of Clifton............Clifton, N. J.
1966.... Dayton Boys' Club....East Dayton Branch, Ohio
1967.... Dayton Boys' Club.............Dayton, Ohio

TEAM CHAMPIONS—INTERMEDIATE DIVISION

1956 .... Albany Boys' Club, Inc .... Albany, N. Y.
1957 .... Boys' Club of Princeton, Inc .... Princeton, Ind.
        R. W. Brown Boys' Club .... Philadelphia, Pa.
1958 .... Boys' Club of New York ...... New York, N. Y.
        Tompkins Square Branch
1959 .... Variety International Boys' Club
                                  Los Angeles, Calif.
1960 .... Variety International Boys' Club
                                  Los Angeles, Calif.
1961 .... Boys' Club of Pittsburgh .... Pittsburgh, Pa.
1962 .... Variety Boys' Club .... Los Angeles, Calif.
1963 .... Boys' Club of Santa Ana ..... Santa Ana, Calif.
1964 .... Boys' Club of Queens ... Long Island City, N. Y.
1965 .... Boys' Club of Pittsburgh .... Pittsburgh, Pa.
1966 .... Boys' Club of Virginia Peninsula
                              Newport News, Virginia
1967 .... Boys' Club of Niagara Falls
                              Niagara Falls, New York

TEAM CHAMPIONS—SENIOR DIVISION

1961 .... Boys' Club of Pittsburgh .... Pittsburgh, Pa.
1962 .... Variety Boys' Club .... Los Angeles, Calif.
1963 .... Boys' Club of Pittsburgh .... Pittsburgh, Pa.
1964 .... Boys' Club of Pittsburgh .... Pittsburgh, Pa.
1965 .... Boys' Club of Queens ... Long Island City, N. Y.
1966 .... Boys' Club of Pittsburgh .... Pittsburgh, Pa.
1967 .... Boys' Club of Queens ... Long Island City, N. Y.

POCKET BILLIARD
TOURNAMENTS (1961-1967)

Johnston City, Illinois World's All-Round

All-Round		Pockets
1961 . .		
1962 . .	Luther Lassiter	Luther Lassiter
1963 . .	Luther Lassiter	Luther Lassiter
1964 . .	Eddie Taylor	Luther Lassiter
1965 . .	Harold Worst	Harold Worst
1965 . .	Joe Balsis	Joe Balsis
1967 . .	Luther Lassiter	Irving Crane

One Pocket		Nine Ball
1961 . .	John Vevis	
1962 . .	Marshall Carpenter	Luther Lassiter
1963 . .	Eddie Taylor	Luther Lassiter
1964 . .	Eddie Taylor	Luther Lassiter
1965 . .	Larry Johnson	Harold Worst
1966 . .	Ed Kelly	Ed Kelly
1967 . .	Larry Johnson	Luther Lassiter

Las Vegas, Nevada World's All-Round (Open)

All-Round	Pockets
1965 . . Harold Worst	Irving Crane

One Pocket	Nine Ball
Harold Worst	Ed Kelley

All-Round	Pockets
1966 . . Ronnie Allen	Cicero Murphy

One Pocket	Nine Ball
Larry Johnson	Ronnie Allen

All-Round	Pockets
1967 . . Eddie Taylor	Mike Eufemia

One Pocket	Nine Ball
Eddie Taylor	Danny Jones

Long Beach, California International Open Pocket Billiard Tournament

All-Round	Pockets
1967 . . Luther Lassiter	Lasser Lassiter

One Pocket	Nine Ball
Ed Kelly	Joe Balsis

Burbank, California World's Invitational 14.1 Championships

1965 . . Cicero Murphy (17-3)
            Runner-up—Luther Lassiter (16-4)
1966 . . Joe Balsis   (15-2)
            Runner-up—Willie Mosconi (14-3)

Billiard Room Proprietor Association of America
New York City World's Invitational 14.1 Championships

1963 . . Luther Lassiter (10-1) High run George Chenier (150).
1964 . . Luther Lassiter (10-3) Won Playoff over Art Cranfield (150-44) High Run Canfield (141).
1965 . . Joe Balsis (12-2) High Run—Irving Crane (120).
1966 . . Luther Lassiter (11-3) Won playoff over Cicero Murphy (150-111). High Run—Irving Crane (141).
1967 . . Luther Lassiter (12-2) Runner-up Jack Briet High Run—Joe Balsis (143)

BCA "Player of the Year" Money Winners Computed on Participation in BCA Sanctioned Tournaments only

A. E. Schmidt Top Dollar Award $2,500
                    . . .Luther Lassiter $7,500
Tweeten Fibre Co. Inc. Award $500
                    . . .Joe Balsis $4,800
Bud Hobbs $250
                    . . .Jack Breit $4,300
Ewald Fischer Co. Award $1,000
                    . . .Dorothy Wise $ 650

1967 U. S. OPEN FINALISTS
STATE AND "METRO" CHAMPIONS

DOUBLE ELIMINATION

June 26-30, 1967—Sheraton-Jefferson, St. Louis, Missouri
MEN

STATE	TOURN. SITE	CHAMPION	HOME TOWN
Arkansas	Little Rock	Vernon K. Brown	Little Rock, Ark.
Connecticut	Stratford	Angelo Caramanica	Stratford, Conn.
Hawaii	Honolulu	Joseph P. Quiyote	Honolulu, Hawaii

STATE	TOURN. SITE	CHAMPION	HOME TOWN
Illinois	Collinsville	Frank Tullos	Belleville, Ill.
Illinois	Rockford	William P. Spencer	Morton Grove, Ill.
Indiana	Crawfordsville	Steve Mizerak	Anderson, Ind.
Iowa	Iowa City	Maynard Parish	Monmouth, Ill.
Michigan	Lansing	Tom Kollins	Westland, Mich.
Michigan	Livonia (Detroit)	Alton Whitlow	Detroit, Mich.
Minnesota	Minneapolis	William White	Minneapolis, Minn.
Mississippi	Jackson	T. J. Springer	Mantee, Miss.
Missouri	Florissant	Ardell Le Sieur	River View, Mo.
Missouri	St. Louis	James Gordon	St. Louis, Mo.
New York	Flushing	Stanley Morycz	Brooklyn, N. Y.
North Carolina	Roxboro	James Acree	Roanoke Rapids, N. C.
North Dakota	Fargo	John Canal	Minot A.F. Sta., N.D.
Pennsylvania	Hanover	Clair E. Fry	York, Pa.
Texas	El Paso	Thomas E. Gold	El Paso, Texas
Texas	Ft. Worth	U. J. Puckett	Ft. Worth, Texas
Wisconsin	Milwaukee	Charles Stone	Kenosha, Wis.

INVITEES

1966 U. S. Open	Irving Crane	Rochester, N. Y.
Long Beach 9-Ball	Joe Balsis	Minersville, Penn.
Long Beach One-Pocket	Ed Kelly	Las Vegas, Nevada
Long Beach Straight	Luther Lassiter	Elizabeth City, N. J.

WOMEN'S DIVISION
1967 U. S. OPEN FINALISTS STATE CHAMPIONS
DOUBLE ELIMINATION
June 26-30, 1967—Sheraton-Jefferson, St. Louis, Missouri
WOMEN

STATE	TOURN. SITE	CHAMPION	HOME TOWN
California	Mountain View	Dorthoy Wise	Redwood City, Calif.
Illinois	Collinsville	Vivian Scott	St. Louis, Mo.
Indiana	Crawfordsville	Shelia Bohm	Home Ct.
			Rochester, Ind.
Kansas	At Large	Betty Jo Hember	Lawrence, Kansas
Maryland	Silver Springs	Christ Miller	Landover, Md.
Michigan	Lansing—(66)	Jeane Ann Williams	Lansing, Mich.
Michigan	Lansing—(67)	Jackie Gorecki	Grand Rapids, Mich.
Michigan	Livonia (Detroit)	Chari Fate	Williamston, Mich.
Missouri	St. Louis	Kathy Bruton	Ballwin, Missouri
Missouri	At Large	San Lynn Merrick	Kansas City, Mo.
Ohio	At Large	Geraldine Titcomb	Cincinnati, Ohio
Texas	At Large	Susan Sloan	Beaumont, Texas

1967 U. S. OPEN RANKING
OF PLAYERS FINISHING IN THE MONEY
MEN'S DIVISION

Rank		Prize	Balls Per Inning Average
1	Jimmy Caras	$3,000	11.02
2	Luther Lassiter ...	2,000	6.86
3	Irving Crane	1,500	9.29
4	Dallas West	1,250	8.26
5	Johnny Ervolino ..	1,000	7.00
6	Jack Breit	900	6.66
7	Joe Balsis	800	10.70
8	Frank McGown	700	6.86
9	Steve Mizerak	600	9.23
10	Dan Gartner	500	8.16
11	Alton Whitlow	400	6.66
12	Maynard Parish ...	300	4.81
13	Lou Butera	250	10.05
14	Cisero Murphy	200	7.96

Each of the following received $100: Charles Stone, balls per inning average, 6.91; Bob Noland, 4.50; Danny DiLiberto, 4.96; A Caramanica, 5.49; Mike Eufemia, 5.90; U. J. Puckett, 5.94; Stan Morycz, 6.08; Billy Staton, 6.86; Ed Kelly, 8.20; Ardell LeSieur, 4.62; T. J. Springer, 4.74.
High Run Out of the Money—Tom Kollins, 65, $300.
High Run in the Money—Dallas West, 113, $200.

WOMEN'S DIVISION

			Balls Per Inning
1	Dorothy Wise	$500	2.36
2	San Lynn Merrick	300	2.03
3	Sheila Bohm	200	1.46

High Run Out of the Money—Jeanne Ann Williams, 28, $200.
High Run in the Money—Dorothy Wise, 40, $100.